The Roman Chilterns

by
Keith Branigan
and
Rosalind Niblett

First published in the UK by

The Chess Valley Archaeological and Historical Society
Chesham, Bucks.

ISBN 0 9516345 5 0

Copy editing by
Lena Woldemariam, Josephine Campbell and Clare Butler

Layout by Lena Woldemariam

Cover design by Blank Designs

Printed by Ashford Colour Press

About the authors

Professor Keith Branigan is a native of Chesham and was a founder member of the CVAHS, directing the excavations at Latimer villa between 1964 and 1970.

He took a BA in Ancient History and Archaeology at the University of Birmingham where he also took his PhD and was a Research Fellow. He was appointed Lecturer in Archaeology at the University of Bristol in 1966 and Professor of Prehistory and Archaeology at the University of Sheffield in 1976.

His previous publications include *Town and Country: The Archaeology of the Roman Chilterns* and *The Catuvellauni* in *The People of Roman Britain* series, of which he is the Editor.

Dr Rosalind Niblett was brought up at Chorleywood and read Archaeology at Cardiff University. After working as a Field Archaeologist in Essex and Bucks, she returned to Hertfordshire in 1971 and, since then, has worked as an Archaeologist based at St Albans.

She has directed numerous excavations and published nearly 50 articles and books, mainly on Romano-British topics, which is the area in which she specialises. She is currently the District Archaeologist for St Albans District Council.

Acknowledgements

The Chess Valley Archaeological and Historical Society wishes to thank the authorities at the St Albans Museums for their kind permission to use their photograph of the mosaic showing the horned god on the front cover, and also for the use of the drawings and illustrations in Chapters 3 and 4 of this book, namely:

- The Beech Bottom Dyke. Photo – Simon West, © St Albans Museums.
- A mid-first century iron *lorica* with bronze fittings found just outside the Roman town – drawing by Philip Dean.
- Iron mail from the chieftain's burial at Folly Lane, © St Albans Museums.
- Bronze cheek piece and bridle bit; both inlaid with enamel from the chieftain's burial at Folly Lane, © St Albans Museums.
- The reconstructed cross-section of the structures associated with the chieftain's burial at Folly Lane. Drawing – Alex Thorne © St Albans Museums.
- Grave offerings from a burial just outside Verulamium and dating from approximately AD 85, © St Albans Museums.
- Leather off-cuts from a late first-century rubbish dump and an iron wool-carding comb from the Gorhambury villa, © St Albans Museums.
- A collection of iron tips for ploughshares. All were found in Verulamium and underline the importance of agriculture to the town's inhabitants, © St Albans Museums.
- Mithras, the Persian god of light, as depicted on a late second-century beaker found in Verulamium, © St Albans Museums.
- Bronze statuette of Mercury accompanied by his traditional attributes, a ram, a cock and a tortoise, © St Albans Museums.
- Sir Mortimer Wheeler excavating the shell mosaic in 1930, © St Albans Museums.
- Painted wall plaster from a mid-second-century house, © St Albans Museums.
- A 'hunt cup' decorated with hares and hounds, third century, © St Albans Museums.
- The face of a wealthy third-century citizen of Verulamium. Reconstructed by Richard Neave from the remarkably well-preserved skeleton buried in a lead coffin, © St Albans Museums.
- The third-century town walls, © St Albans Museums.
- Post holes outlining an early post-Roman wooden building outside the north-east gate of Verulamium, © St Albans Museums.

CONTENTS

Introduction

Keith Branigan

This small book has been produced to meet the ongoing demand for an introduction to, and an overview of, the archaeology and history of the Chilterns during the period of the Roman occupation of Britain. Much of that demand has been stimulated by the continuing series of excavations and discoveries in modern St Albans. St Albans, or Verulamium as it was called by the Romans, was one of the most important and 'romanised' cities in the Roman province of Britannia.

The story of Roman Verulamium has been told and illustrated in some detail in Rosalind Niblett's recent book *Verulamium: The Roman City of St Albans* (Tempus 2001). This book attempts to place Verulamium in its contemporary context, and to trace the history not only of the city but also of the countryside around it.

The relationship between town and country was an important one. The town was the seat of local government, whose writ extended across the Chilterns and beyond. It was also the place where imported and manufactured goods could most easily be acquired, and Roman entertain-ments could be enjoyed. But the town depended on the countryside for most of its food supply, and many of the families who filled the ranks of the local council actually lived in the countryside or had an estate there.

The story of the Roman Chilterns was presented by the same authors in 1994, as two chapters of *The Archaeology of the Chilterns* (CVAHS 1994). That book is now out of print, but interest in the archaeology of the Chilterns in general, and of the Roman Chilterns in particular, continues unabated. The CVAHS, therefore, decided to issue a smaller volume on the Roman period, based on the two chapters of the earlier book. The chapters on Verulamium have been updated and rewritten by Rosalind Niblett, and that on the countryside has been revised and formed into two chapters by Keith Branigan.

We hope that *The Roman Chilterns* will provide an interesting and stimulating introduction to the story of the Chilterns during the four centuries in which they were part of the Roman Empire.

Chapter 1
From Caesar to Cunobelin

Keith Branigan

The Roman Chilterns describes both the period of time with which we are concerned, and the legal status of the Chilterns during that period – part of a conquered native kingdom, now incorporated into a Roman province. But it was a region that was occupied, of course, even during the Roman period, largely by Britons who belonged to a tribe called the Catuvellauni.

The origins of the tribe are shrouded in mystery, and they are not amongst the 11 'Belgic' tribes referred to by Julius Caesar in his account of his British expeditions in 55 and 54 BC. There is no doubt that Caesar marched his troops into the Chilterns in 54 BC, crossing the Thames and attempting unsuccessfully to bring Cassivellaunus, the British leader, to battle.

Even before Caesar's intervention Cassivellaunus had apparently been continually at war with the neighbouring tribes. It appears that the middle of the first century BC was a period when small tribal units in southern Britain were constantly engaged in warfare in attempts to assert themselves and extend their territory and their economic base. In 55/54 BC Cassivellaunus and his people seem to have emerged as one of the more successful tribes, already putting pressure on the Trinovantes of Essex who controlled much of the lucrative cross-channel trade with Gaul and Rome.

Although Cassivellaunus disappears from history after Caesar's expeditions, a powerful new tribal kingdom grew up over the next three decades. By 20 BC, under King Tasciovanus, it controlled Hertfordshire, much of Buckinghamshire, Bedfordshire, and Oxfordshire east of the Cherwell. His capital was now established at Verulamium, where he minted gold coins and established trading if not diplomatic links with the Romans. Roman trade goods – fine pottery and glass, bronze and silver vessels, and amphorae full of wine – flowed into Verulamium, and into the hands of the upper echelons of tribal society.

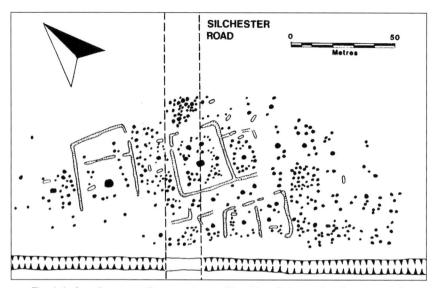

Fig. 1.1 A native cremation cemetery at King Harry's Lane, St Albans, used for burials from c.10 BC to AD 45.

Caesar describes native British society as essentially comprising two classes – the *equites,* or nobles, and the peasants. This is graphically represented at Verulamium by the cremation cemetery of 15 BC – AD 45, in which a series of ditched enclosures, each containing a central burial accompanied by a wealth of grave goods, is surrounded by dozens of simple cremations with few grave goods or none at all (fig. 1.1). The richest burials, however, are found in the countryside, particularly around the Welwyn area, where single cremations in deep pits are surrounded by remarkable displays of wealth.

At Panshanger, for example, the cremation was accompanied by five amphorae of wine, 36 other pottery vessels, a silver cup (fig. 1.2), a bronze serving dish and strainer, and a set of 24 glass gaming pieces. Around this burial,

Fig. 1.2 A silver cup from a wealthy cremation burial at Panshanger.

as at Verulamium, were at least half a dozen cremations with few grave goods or none at all.

Traces of a contemporary settlement site were found only 150 metres from the Panshanger burial, and the rural 'Welwyn-type' cremation sites are probably the burial places of wealthy members of the tribal elite who lived on farms spread across parts of the tribal territory. The focus of these farms seems to have been an oval or sometimes a rectangular ditched and palisaded enclosure with one or two circular timber-framed houses inside. Occasional fragments of amphorae, imported pottery and glass, slave chains

Fig. 1.4 A gold coin of the Catuvellaunian King Cunobelin.

(fig. 1.3) and coins belie the apparent 'poverty' of these farms.

Under Tasciovanus' successor, Cunobelin, the Catuvellauni continued their growth and expansion. By AD 10 Cunobelin had seized the Trinovantian capital of Camulodunum (Colchester). With the Catuvellauni in control of Essex, trade with the Roman world expanded further, and alongside the previous imports, new and more exotic products were acquired – olive oil, fish sauces, and the attractive Arretine pottery made in Italy and southern Gaul.

Cunobelin seems to have shifted his capital to Camulodunum and was minting his own coins there (fig. 1.4). Many of his coins, particularly those circulating in the Catuvellaunian heartland of

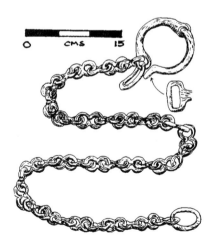

Fig. 1.3 A slave chain found in a pit alongside a pre-Roman timber hut at Park Street, south of St Albans.

Hertfordshire and Buckinghamshire, carry the legend TASC.FIL (son of Tasciovanus) on their reverse. By the time he died around AD 40 his coins were to be found over an area today occupied by more than a dozen counties, and there is some reason to think that brothers and sons had been installed to rule newly conquered territories.

When Cunobelin died, the Catuvellaunian kingdom may have been divided in two, between the two sons who succeeded him – Togodumnus and Caratacus. They had scarcely taken the reins of power when they were confronted by a full-scale Roman invasion.

Chapter 2
The Impact of Rome
Keith Branigan

The dynastic struggles in Britain that followed the death of the great Cunobelin provided the pretext for the new Roman emperor, Claudius, to undertake the invasion of Britain. He did so largely for political reasons, but it was no light undertaking. The Roman army of invasion consisted of four legions and a similar number of auxiliaries – about 50,000 men in all. Togodumnus and Caratacus, the sons of Cunobelin, who had probably divided his kingdom between them, attempted to meet and defeat the invaders in Kent, but both were beaten, and the British fell back to the Thames. Here they hoped to find a secure position on the northern bank, but they were outflanked and overwhelmed in fierce fighting, and Togodumnus died shortly after, presumably of wounds acquired in battle.

While the Romans awaited the arrival of Claudius himself, the British seem to have regrouped and placed themselves between the Roman bridgehead and the line of advance towards Camulodunum (Colchester), where Cunobelin had established his capital. However, they were no match for the legions, and they seem to have retreated and conceded defeat rather than face annihilation. And so the Roman army swung eastwards, and for the moment the Chilterns avoided the rapacity of the Roman army on the march.

Claudius advanced to Camulodunum and there received the submission of British chieftains, amongst whom, we must assume, were representatives of the Catuvellauni – both those based at Camulodunum and those who still looked to Verulamium as their focus.

Their surviving king, Caratacus, however, was not among them, having eluded the Romans and escaped westwards. He reappears five or six years later, leading the Welsh resistance to the Romans. We are told by the Roman historian, Tacitus, that he won many battles and that his fame reached as far as Rome itself.

When he was finally captured in AD 52 and taken to Rome, we are given by Tacitus a version (no doubt fanciful) of what this Catuvellaunian prince and king, who in his youth would have seen Verulamium and frequently travelled through the Chilterns, said to Claudius:

"I owned horses, men, weapons and wealth. Are you surprised I regret losing them? If you wish to rule the world, should you expect everyone else to welcome slavery?"

Fanciful or not, his speech holds a special fascination as the first recorded words of a man of the Chilterns. Claudius approved and pardoned Caratacus, who lived out his life in Rome – a long way from his native hills.

Meanwhile, his former subjects had soon come under the direct control of the Roman army, although the rapidity of the Roman advance and the apparent pacification of the Chilterns at least meant that the invading forces left few troops to garrison the area. Indeed, the only possible fort that we know of in the Chilterns may have been built at Verulamium, housing about 500 men.

Bronze fittings from military uniforms have been found at Braughing to the east and Northchurch to the west, but no traces of forts have yet been found there. Otherwise, the nearest forts were well to the north and northwest of the hills at Godmanchester and possibly Little Brickhill.

The people of the Chilterns, therefore, apart from those living in or close to the tribal centre at Verulamium, would have come into direct contact with the Romans only slowly and infrequently. Just how quickly the Romans were able to impose taxes on the native farmers and collect them is unclear, but they may have relied (as in other provinces) on civilian tax collectors rather than the army to carry out the task. In any event, any garrison at Verulamium was not long imposed on the locals, for around AD 49 there was a major redeployment of troops, who were moved westwards to the River Severn.

The nucleus of a romanised town, with a grid of streets, was laid out in the AD 50s, and it is described in greater detail in the following chapter. Together with the contemporary founding of a

Roman colony at Camulodunum (Colchester) and the creation of a civilian settlement at London, the new Verulamium provided a boost to the process of romanising the native population.

Boudica in the Chilterns

When their neighbours, the Trinovantes and the Iceni, joined together under Queen Boudica in revolt against Rome in AD 60/61, the Catuvellauni significantly did not join them. In fact, after sacking Colchester and London, the rebels marched on Verulamium and burnt down the new town, which was mostly still built of timber. They no doubt followed the new road from London northwards and attacked farms and settlements in south Hertfordshire on the way. At Park Street, just south of Verulamium, the house of a Chiltern farmer was totally destroyed, and a similar fate befell the farm at Gorhambury, just north of the new town.

The new town was itself razed to the ground. Whilst the rest of the countryside was bypassed by the dissidents, a further group may have sailed up the Thames, or marched west along its north bank, and attacked another new settlement at Staines, known as

Pontibus, because it was the site of a bridge over the river.

When the rebels had finally been defeated, the Romans brought some troops back to garrison the area, but again the Chilterns seem to have been regarded as pacified, and new temporary forts were established at Dorchester on Thames, Little Brickhill and Great Chesterford, forming an arc around the Chilterns from west to east.

Confidence was slow to recover after the destruction and slaughter of AD 60/61, and both at Verulamium and in the Chiltern valleys rebuilding and redevelopment was piecemeal.

Devolution – Local Self-government

A major change took place sometime in the mid 70s under the Emperor Vespasian. He had been commander of the Legion II Augusta in AD 43 and so had taken part in the invasion of Britain. Now, as emperor, he chose to bestow local self-government on some of the former native kingdoms in south-east England.

A number of self-governing local authorities, called *civitates*, were created to administer law and order, to be responsible for tax collection and the maintenance of roads within their territory, and generally to act as a lower tier of government below the governor of the province. They were the equivalent of county councils today, but they were responsible for much larger areas, based mostly on the old tribal territories.

The Chilterns lay at the heart of the former tribal kingdom of the Catuvellauni, and so they found themselves as the focus of the new *civitas*. Westwards, it stretched into Oxfordshire, with its border at the Cherwell; northwards, it reached well into Northamptonshire, probably to the Welland Valley, while to the east it incorporated Bedfordshire and Hertfordshire and parts of Huntingdonshire and Cambridgeshire. This enormous area, some 4,000 square miles, had to have an administrative capital, and Verulamium was the obvious choice.

Over the next few decades the town developed rapidly, as the public buildings necessary for the capital of a *civitas* were erected, and privately owned shops and taverns were built to serve the needs of residents and visitors

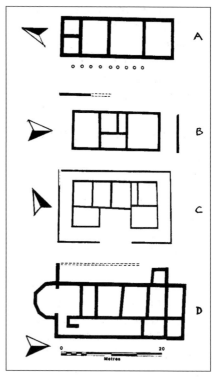

Fig. 2.1 The floor plans of late first century villas at a) Lockleys, b) Park Street, c) Boxmoor, d) Gorhambury.

alike. Initially, however, it is significant that private houses in Verulamium lagged behind those being built in the Chiltern valleys in terms of the facilities and comforts they provided.

Villas – farmhouses which reflected the taste for romanised living – were being built, not only just outside Verulamium at Park Street and Gorhambury, but further afield at Lockleys, Boxmoor (fig.

9

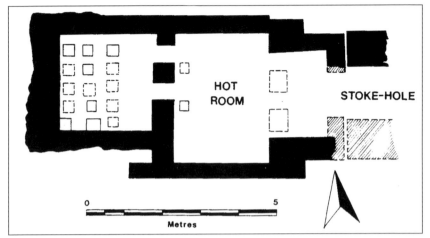

HOT ROOM

STOKE-HOLE

0   5

Metres

Fig. 2.2 A first-century bathhouse serving the occupants of the Park Street villa.

2.1), Gadebridge, Saunderton and Hambleden.

Even in the later first century, most of these villas had stone and mortar walls or footings, tiled roofs, and good solid floors of mortar or even coarse plain mosaic surfaces made up of thousands of tile cubes. Walls were mostly plastered and usually painted in simple rectilinear panels. The houses each had four, five or six separate rooms, accessed independently from a corridor or verandah, providing both privacy and the opportunity to use different rooms for different activities. At least two of these early villas, at Park Street and Gadebridge, also had free-standing bathhouses which, though small, provided the basic range of cold, warm and hot rooms (fig. 2.2).

All in all, these new farmhouses were very different from the timber houses that had stood on these sites at the time of the Roman invasion. All of these early villas lay on or close to existing communications or early Roman roads.

In the heart of the western Chilterns, in the valleys of the Chess and Misbourne, there were no such routes to take advantage of at this time, but new farms, whose occupiers used mostly native-style pottery, began to appear in the last decades of the first century AD.

At Latimer part of a large and sturdy timber farmhouse was

excavated; but at other sites like Sarratt, Great Missenden and Shardeloes we presently have only the evidence of the pottery to go on. Nevertheless, the evidence suggests an expansion of farming into valleys that had previously been little utilised in the preceding centuries. Once a road could be provided through the Chilterns, linking these valleys both to Verulamium and to the Thames, they too could expect to see the building of villas.

The Romans were justly famous for their roads, and because roads were required early in the conquest to facilitate the movement of troops and their supplies, roads which ran north – south through the Chilterns, like Watling Street and Ermine Street, were built and available for civilian traffic within a few years of AD 43. These major strategic roads were about 10 metres wide, often with substantial foundations, a gravelled surface and flanking drainage ditches. They were built to carry heavy traffic, and they were built to last. They provided a crucial link between major towns like London and Verulamium.

Along these trunk roads sped couriers from the governor and his officials in London, and at a more leisurely pace went the census officials and tax collectors. The local authorities through whose territory they passed were responsible for maintaining posting stations and inns along these routes.

Watling Street was particularly important, as it provided a reliable link between the port of London and the tribal capital and its market place at Verulamium. From Verulamium it ran on north-westwards through Dunstable and other small settlements towards the West Midlands. At the eastern end of the Chilterns the forerunner of the Great North Road, Ermine Street, ran from London through Enfield and Braughing on its way to Lincoln and eventually York. From Verulamium Akeman Street branched off westwards along the valley of the Bulbourne, passing through the town of Alchester on its route to Cirencester (fig. 2.3).

Before the end of the first century the Lower Icknield Way had been formalised into an east – west road varying between 4 and 7 metres wide, which ran along the foot of the Chiltern escarpment. This road provided an important link between the farming estates on the edge of the clay vale and the towns of Dorchester, Dunstable and Baldock.

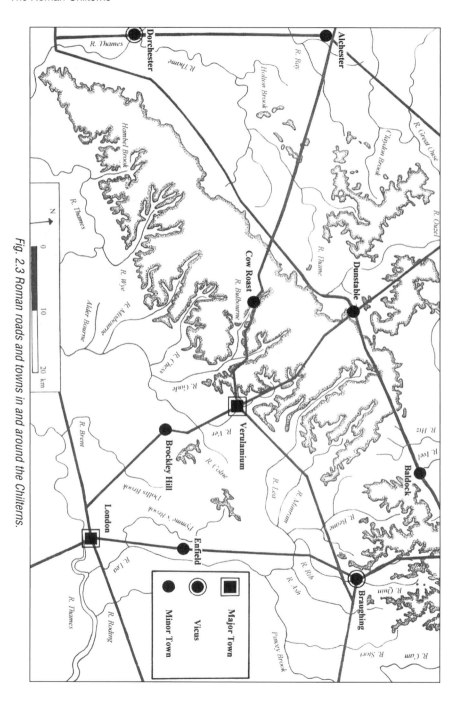

Fig. 2.3 Roman roads and towns in and around the Chilterns.

In the early second century the road from Braughing to Verulamium was extended westwards through the valleys of the Chess, Misbourne and Wye to provide a link between the farms in these valleys, Verulamium to the east and the river Thames at Hedsor to the west. From the start these secondary roads would have been the responsibility of the local *civitas*, and their construction emphasises the importance that the *civitas* and its landowners and farmers placed on providing a link between town and country.

Market Towns for Chiltern Farmers

Apart from Verulamium, which was obviously a major commercial centre with a large market place, a market hall and dozens of shops, there were no Roman towns in the Chiltern valleys – but there were several around the fringes of the hill country.

Just beyond the escarpment lay Baldock, Dunstable and Dorchester, strung along the Lower Icknield Way. Baldock was a settlement of some importance in the years before the Roman invasion, and it subsequently grew to be a sprawling settlement of 50 to 70 acres (20-30 hectares). Its several extensive cemeteries suggest a large population, most of whom appear to have continued to live in timber buildings with few romanised pretensions. But there were some houses with hypocaust-heated living or bath-rooms and with painted plaster on

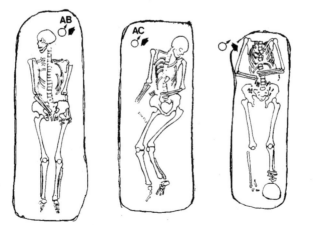

Fig. 2.4 Four of the burials in the Roman cemetery of the small town at Durocobrivae (Dunstable).

13

their walls. The population was probably mainly engaged in farming on the surrounding land, and if the Romano-Celtic temple identified on aerial photographs was excavated, one suspects it would prove to be dedicated to a deity associated with farming and animals.

Dunstable, which the Romans called Durocobrivae, was a similar but probably smaller settlement. Its appearance in no less than three of the itineraries of the imperial post implies that there was a posting station there, although its location is yet unknown. Being situated on Watling Street, one of the great trunk roads of the province, it must have seen many travellers and have possessed some taverns and hostels to serve their needs, but these too remain to be discovered.

At present the numerous wells and corn-drying ovens and the discovery of ploughshares and sickles in the town confirm that it was home to a substantial agrarian population, some of whom were buried in the town cemetery (fig. 2.4). It no doubt also served as a local market centre for the nearby rural population, providing services such as iron and bronze smithing and wood-working to local farms.

The grave of one local carpenter was found in the cemetery with an inscribed drinking cup (fig. 2.5), donated on behalf of his guild at Verulamium. Since he died in his late teens, he can have been little more than an apprentice.

Further west, beyond the western tip of the Chilterns, where the

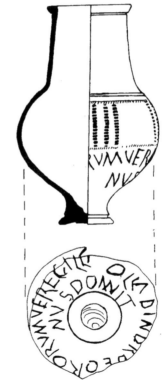

Fig. 2.5 A cup found in the grave of a carpenter, Regillinus, buried by his fellow guild-members at Dunstable.

14

hills are cut by the Goring Gap, a third town developed at Dorchester on Thames. This had been the location of an important pre-Roman settlement. Once the temporary fort established after the Boudican revolt was demolished, a small market town seems to have developed quite rapidly. A gravelled square near the centre of the town may have served as a market place, where both local farm produce and manufactured goods, conveniently and cheaply shipped up river, were sold or exchanged.

The townspeople lived in timber-framed buildings, and even in its later history there were as yet few signs of architectural pretensions in its private houses. Yet in spite of this and its small size – less than 15 acres (6 hectares) – there are indications that Dorchester was a town of some local importance. Towards the end of the second century it was provided with an earth rampart for defence, and before the end of the third century this had been fronted by a stone wall.

An altar found here suggests the presence of a temple, perhaps dedicated to Jupiter, but is also of interest because it was erected by one Marcus Varius Severus, who is described as a 'beneficiarius consularis'. He probably would have been a legionary seconded to the staff of the governor in London to help with provincial administration. Whether he was just passing through Dorchester or not we do not know, but it is likely in any case that Dorchester served a local administrative role, here, at the south-western corner of the *civitas*, a long way from Verulamium.

At the opposite end of the Chilterns, at Braughing, was an important road junction where Ermine Street, running north to Lincoln and York, crossed the road linking the Roman colony at Colchester to the town of Verulamium. Roman Braughing appears to have been about the same size as Baldock, 60 to 75 acres (24-30 hectares), but to have been a town of greater status. It possessed several buildings which are likely to have been public rather than private, though most are known from survey and sample excavations rather than full investigation.

A courtyard building with an outer yard, the whole complex covering an area about 65 by 30 metres, looks very much like a public inn or *mansio*, whilst a large L-shaped building alongside the street may have been a market hall.

Down by the river there was a small bathhouse, whilst at least three other large buildings with stone foundations are known in the town. Taken together with the evidence for timber-built shops, the impression emerges of a thriving market town and minor administrative centre here on the eastern border of the *civitas*.

Rural Industry in the Roman Chilterns

The small towns were home to a variety of craftsmen, like the young carpenter from Dunstable, but industrial activities – involving the extraction of raw materials and the mass production of goods by a team of workers – were mostly confined to rural locations.

Iron-working was never as important in the Chilterns as it was further north in the *civitas* in Northamptonshire, but two settlements in which it appears to have played a significant role were Cow Roast in the Bulbourne valley and Foxholes near Hertford.

Many bowl furnaces have been found at Cow Roast, and it is likely that the iron-workers here were exploiting local 'bog ore'. Little is known of the settlement itself – a few areas of chalk floor, a number of postholes and several wells – but it appears to have its origins in a pre-Roman iron-working site. Foxholes is also poorly known, but has already yielded the remains of over 40 bowl furnaces and ore roasting ovens. Settlements like these may have seen a certain amount of secondary working – smithing – as well as supplying smelted iron to the blacksmiths in Verulamium and elsewhere.

The towns would also have been prime markets for tile producers, with so many buildings clustered together all using clay tiles on their roofs. The quantity needed in Verulamium, and the cost of transporting such heavy products any distance, meant that there must have been tileries in the immediate vicinity of the town, but they have yet to be found. They are known further afield at Aldenham, Edgware and Little Hadham and on the villa estates at Netherwild and Park Street, just south of Verulamium.

These villa-based tile kilns might reasonably be thought to have been producing for use on the estate itself, and no doubt they were, but they were also well-

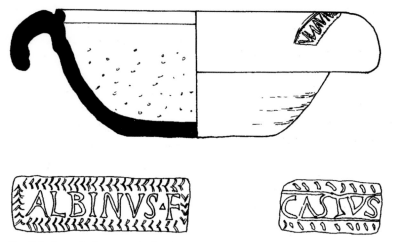

Fig. 2.6 A mortarium or grinding bowl made in the potteries at Brockley Hill, and two of the manufacturers' name stamps.

placed to send tiles to Verulamium. It may therefore be significant that the Netherwild kilns, making both roofing and hypocaust tiles, were producing in the mid-second century, when there was extensive reconstruction in Verulamium following the fire around AD 155. Similarly the large tile kiln at Park Street was built around AD 300, when, not only the villa, but also the nearby town were undergoing renovation and new building. The kilns may have produced a useful, if short-lived, supplement to the income from farming.

It is possible that farmers were also involved in pottery production on a seasonal basis, producing the basic range of pots – storage jars, bowls, flagons and dishes – in grey or buff wares. The south Buckinghamshire kilns at Hedgerley and Fulmer supplied pots to the villas in the adjacent valleys, but not, it seems, to any major towns. The demand may therefore have been met by relatively casual seasonal production rather than full-time activity. The same may be true of the Hadham kilns near Braughing.

The kilns at Brockley Hill and Radlett were a very different proposition. They specialised in producing the big heavy grinding bowls known as *mortaria* (fig. 2.6), and they exported their products over much of southern Britain in the first and second centuries. Because they stamped their names, like a trademark, on the rims of their *mortaria*, we know the names of some of these successful entrepreneurs – Oastrius, Secundus and Castus. The most prolific of them all, Albinus, was followed in the business by his son, Matugenus.

They were probably all industrial tenants of the man who owned the potting fields at Brockley Hill, as its Roman name was Sulloniacis, which means 'the estate of Sullonius'.

Chapter 3

The Roman City of Verulamium

Rosalind Niblett

A kilometre south-west of the medieval and modern town of St Albans is the site of Verulamium, once one of the largest walled towns in the Roman province of Britannia. Today little is visible of the town apart from remnants of the third-century town wall, the foundations of the great gateway through which travellers from London entered the town, the theatre, and a handful of private houses and shops. Air photography, however, tells a different story, revealing an extensive grid of streets, with houses, temples and workshops extending over 200 acres (40 hectares). Above all, the Verulamium Museum, close to the site of the Roman Forum, houses a wealth of mosaics, painted wall plaster, pottery and metalwork demonstrating a level of sophistication equal to that from any other Romano-British town in the province.

The origins of Verulamium, however, lie some time before the arrival of the Roman conquest in AD 43. Towards the end of the first century BC there seems to have been a dramatic increase in the number of settlements in the valley of the Ver. Over 20 sites between Park Street and Markyate are now known to have been occupied between about 10 BC and AD 50, and more, no doubt, await discovery.

The thriving population that all this settlement implies was supported by a countryside, which, by the standard of the time, must have been intensively farmed. Pollen preserved in deposits dating from the mid-first century AD suggest that by this time much of the hinterland of Verulamium had been cleared of its forest cover and was devoted to pasture or arable agriculture. Carbonised grains of wheat have been found on several local sites, while the identification as granaries of two timber buildings excavated a short distance outside the Roman town, at Gorhambury, underlines the importance of cereal cultivation.

Alongside this evidence for grain production are traces of stock enclosures and droveways, while animal bones in first-century rubbish tips testify to the raising of pigs, horses, sheep and cattle, with cattle probably increasing in importance at the expense of sheep in the generation before the Roman conquest.

Roman writers tell us that in the first century what is now Hertfordshire lay in the territory of the Catuvellauni, one of the largest and most aggressive tribes in pre-Roman Britain. By the early years of the first century AD the Catuvellaunian ruler, Tasciovanus, was minting coins with the mint mark 'VERUL', implying that Verulamium was already a major centre. In about AD 10 Tasciovanus was succeeded by Cunobelin, perhaps the most successful of all the native kings of pre-Roman Britain. Early in his reign Cunobelin annexed the territory of the neighbouring Trinovantes of Essex and Suffolk and moved his main base to the established Trinovantian capital at Camulodunum, modern Colchester.

Nevertheless, Verulamium remained an important centre: indeed it was during Cunobelin's reign that it enjoyed its greatest wealth. Gold, silver and bronze coins were minted here, and quantities of broken clay moulds in which the coin blanks were cast have been found on several local sites.

It was also under Cunobelin that the area that was to become the centre of the Roman town achieved some sort of special status. A large ditched enclosure, the 'Central Enclosure', is known to underlie the present churchyard and vicarage of St Michael's. This extended over approximately 5 acres (2 hectares) and was surrounded by a massive ditch at least 3 metres deep. A similar ditch running north-east towards the river may have enclosed an annex on its northern side. These ditches pre-date the earliest Roman remains in the area, and it has been suggested that they formed part of an estate centre or royal enclosure occupied by the ruling family.

Of course, pre-Roman Verulamium was not a town in the modern sense of the word. Instead a network of farmsteads spread over an area of at least 3,500 acres (nearly 15 square kilometres) on either side of the River Ver. Traces of eight pre-Roman farmsteads or estate centres have been recorded within 3 kilometres of the centre of the later Roman city. They usually stood within square or

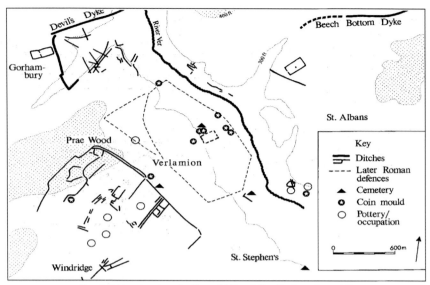

Fig. 3.1 Verulamium in the middle of the first century AD.

rectangular ditched enclosures, surrounded by paddocks, droveways, stockpens and fields. Occasionally out-buildings such as barns, granaries, or workshops have also been recognised (fig. 3.1).

Most of these early farmsteads are only known from air photography, or from finds of pottery or metalwork collected during systematic field surveys. In the 1970s, one such site at Gorhambury, 2 kilometres west of the Roman town, was completely excavated, and this has provided a detailed, and so far unrivalled, picture of a late Iron Age estate.

The main dwelling house stood in an inner enclosure, and measured at least 15 by 4.5 metres with three or four separate rooms. It was flanked by a second house, which may once have had a covered veranda along one side. Remains of a substantial granary and a wooden round house were also recorded, and there may well have been other buildings that were destroyed by later building activity. Traces of gold-working on the site together with exotic imports like Italian wine and grapes point to owners well able to indulge their taste for good living as well as to an extensive trade network. The larger outer compound contained a rectangular aisled building, which was interpreted by the excavators as accommodation for farm-workers and livestock.

Alongside arable farming and stock-raising, iron-working played an important role in the local economy. Fifteen kilometres south of Verulamium extensive deposits of iron ore in the form of nodules of bog iron existed on the slopes of the Chilterns valleys. It is still possible to pick up iron nodules in the fields today, although for commercial purposes the deposits were exhausted before the end of the Roman period. An area of some 40 hectares centred on the Cow Roast pub on the western outskirts of Berkhamsted is known to have been an iron-working centre in the first century AD, while banks and ditches still faintly discernible in the Ashridge Estate above Berkhamsted are all that survives of settlements dating back to the first century. These were constructed by iron-workers and charcoal burners and their families, but do not appear to have been occupied much after the early second century. In the early first century, however, this area of the Chilterns was among the most important iron producing areas in south-eastern England. Verulamium lay across the principal route between this area and the rich late Iron Age communities in north Hertfordshire and Essex, putting the local aristocracy in an ideal position to exploit the iron deposits and to control the trade routes to the north.

A remarkable feature of pre-Roman Verulamium is its apparently peaceable character. This is particularly surprising in view of the impression given by classical writers of a tribal aristocracy dominated by warlords. Admittedly banks and ditches surrounded many of the local farmsteads, but these would have been built more to prevent animals straying and to give the enclosures a certain prestige than for defence. Local burials for the most part lack weapons, although one burial found in what is now Verulamium Park contained an iron spearhead. A number of inlaid horse brasses and a beautifully enamelled lynchpin, probably from a chariot, have also been found locally, while north of Verulamium, at Wheathampstead, inlaid chariot and wagon fittings were being made at about the time of the Roman conquest.

All these are essentially 'showy' objects, however, designed to flaunt the wealth and status of their aristocratic owners – and are

Fig. 3.2 The Beech Bottom Dyke.

the equally massive dyke at Wheathampstead at its northernmost end. The gap between the two earthworks was probably filled with bands of woodland, fences, hedges or trackways, all trace of which has long since vanished.

not necessarily evidence for warfare.

It was at this stage in St Albans' history that the complex system of earthworks on the north, west and south sides of Verulamium was first built. The pattern of these earthworks is not yet fully understood, but in spite of their size they do not appear to have been intended as defence works. The largest of these earthworks is the Beech Bottom Dyke that runs for 2 kilometres on the northern outskirts of the modern town (fig. 3.2).

Beech Bottom Dyke consists of a large ditch with banks on either side. Even today after nearly two thousand years of weathering the ditch is still 10 metres deep. It probably formed part of a territorial boundary running between the valleys of the Lea and the Ver, with

South of the Ver the rather smaller Devil's Dyke near Gorhambury and the dykes south-west of Prae Wood may have delimited the estates of a powerful aristocratic elite. Such an elite would fit in with the descriptions of contemporary society that have come down to us in the writings of classical authors.

Knowledge of the less elevated sections of native society is steadily accumulating. About 150 graves, most of them containing cremations and dating from around 10 BC to AD 55, were excavated in the 1960s in King Harry Lane on the south side of modern St Albans. The accompanying grave goods reflect a group of comfortably off farmers, able to afford occasional imported luxuries in the form of Gaulish tableware or exotic foodstuffs, but who were for the main part content with locally made pottery and modest personal possession such as brooches and box fittings.

AD 43–50:
The Coming of Rome

Cunobelin's long reign came to an end with his death in about AD 40. He was succeeded by two of his sons, Togodumnus and Caratacus, who proved to be less adept in maintaining peaceful relations with Rome.

The newly elevated Emperor Claudius was anxious for a military success with which to enhance his somewhat lacklustre image, and a combination of squabbles among the British aristocracy and alleged British raids on the coasts of Roman Gaul provided him with the necessary pretext for invading Britain in the summer of AD 43.

Many years ago a Roman helmet (with the owner's name, Papirus, stamped on the neck guard) was reputedly found at Verulamium. More recently part of a *lorica* (body armour) was excavated in a rubbish pit just outside the town (fig. 3.3). Both of these objects, together with more than a dozen fragments from other items of

Roman military armour fittings, might suggest the presence here of Roman soldiers at about the time of the conquest. In the past it has been suggested that a Roman fort was established here. At the time of writing, however, no sign of this fort has been found at Verulamium.

There is also a comparative scarcity of coins minted between AD 43 and 64 from Verulamium, and as these are the coins that would have been used by soldiers of the conquest period, their rarity implies that any military presence here was low key and short-lived. A more likely explanation is that

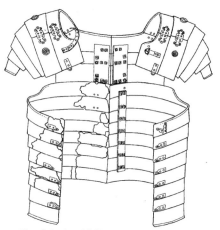

Fig. 3.3 A mid-first century iron lorica *with bronze fittings, found just outside the Roman town.*
The drawing shows a reconstruction of the entire lorica, *with the surviving pieces drawn in heavier lines.*

both the helmet and the *lorica* belonged to native soldiers, returning home after serving as mercenaries in the Roman army, and were deposited on sacred sites as votive offerings to local gods.

If nothing else, however, we can surely assume that the Roman army was responsible for the construction of Watling Street some time in the middle of the first century AD. Watling Street linked Verulamium with the newly established Londinium, and was an essential line of communication for the army as it pressed north-west towards Wales.

No doubt a pre-Roman track existed linking Verulamium with Welwyn and ultimately Colchester, but this must have been properly laid out and surfaced soon after the Roman conquest. Certainly there is evidence to suggest that a causeway was built across the marshy valley floor on the north-east side of Verulamium. Here logs and brushwood, apparently supporting a trackway, were excavated in the early 1960s. It led towards the river, and there may well have already been a bridge at this date.

Apart from road-building. the established, native way of life went on with little sign of change for some years after the Roman invasion. Occupation on the native farmsteads at Park Street and Gorhambury seems to have continued, uninterrupted by the conquest. Certainly the events of AD 43 did not lead to any damage to the property, to any prolonged break in occupation, or even to any change in the use or layout of the buildings, and the ditches in the centre of Verulamium surrounding the putative royal enclosure remained open.

This continuity of native traditions is particularly apparent on an important ceremonial site at Folly Lane on the north side of the valley. Early in the first century AD a farmstead or estate centre had stood here. By the middle of the century this had been swept away and replaced by a large rectangular enclosure surrounded by a ditch 3 metres deep and up to 10 metres wide. Three human skeletons were found in the base of the ditch on one side of the

Fig. 3.4 Iron mail from the chieftain's burial at Folly Lane.

entrance and a deposit of horse and cattle bones on the other. At the centre of the enclosure a large burial pit contained scattered cremated remains, both human and animal. The cremated ashes were accompanied by a large collection of expensive objects. These included a tunic of iron mail (fig. 3.4), enamelled horse equipment (fig. 3.5), remains of an elaborate piece of furniture (possibly a couch) with ivory fittings, and a large quantity of silver. All this material had been burnt, presumably on the funeral pyre, and most of it had been almost completely destroyed.

Fig. 3.5 Bronze cheek piece and bridle bit, both inlaid with enamel, from the chieftain's burial at Folly Lane.

The grave has every appearance of a later Iron Age aristocratic burial, although admittedly one with unusually rich and ostentatious grave offerings. At Folly Lane, however, there was also evidence suggesting that complex and no doubt long-drawn-out rituals had taken place.

The grave itself lay immediately adjacent to an enormous pit, over 12 metres square, in the base of which were the remains of a wooden chamber built nearly 3 metres below the ground. The edges of the pit had been revetted with a double wall of oak or ash, and a narrow walkway or portico surrounded the central chamber (fig. 3.6). In plan the structure was not unlike that of many provincial temples in the Celtic provinces of the Roman Empire.

Similar, although smaller and less elaborate, sunken chambers are known in association with contemporary aristocratic burials at Colchester, where the most likely explanation for them is that they were used during the funerary rites of the local ruling family. A similar interpretation is probably the best one for the Verulamium site, although the enormous size of the enclosure and the complexity of the chamber suggest that it commemorates a tribal leader of exceptional importance.

What the funerary rites involved is very much a matter of speculation, but large quantities of broken tableware and wine jars suggest that they may have included feasting. The ceremonies must

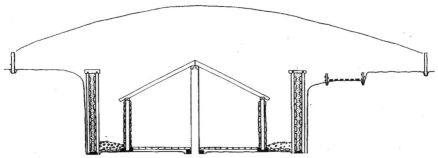

Fig. 3.6 The reconstructed cross-section of the structures associated with the chieftain's burial at Folly Lane. The drawing shows the sturdy wall supporting the vertical sides of the funerary shaft and the funerary chamber on the floor of the shaft. The shallow burial pit lies outside the shaft on the righthand side of the drawing. The roof of the funerary chamber and the mount over both the shaft and the burial pit are entirely hypothetical.

have culminated in the cremation of the body and the grave offerings, and the demolition of the sunken chamber.

By the end of the first century a sizeable Romano-Celtic temple, with flint and mortar foundations, had been built a few metres north-west of the grave and facing towards it. Later on this temple formed part of a much larger religious complex, which only declined with the rise of Christianity at the end of the Roman period.

It is unlikely that the identity of the chieftain at Folly Lane will ever be established, but we can speculate as to the type of person he may have been. He was presumably someone who supported Rome, as it is difficult to imagine the Roman authorities allowing a chieftain opposed to them to maintain his wealth and position in so ostentatious a manner. Indeed, it is conceivable that the Folly Lane chieftain had served in the Roman army or even been educated in Rome.

The practice of taking hostage the sons of native aristocrats in border territories was common in the early Roman Empire. These boys would be brought up and educated in Rome or in a Roman province, and might then serve as officers in auxiliary units in the Roman army. Ultimately they could be sent back to their own lands to promote 'romanisation'.

Assuming that the local chieftain at Verulamium in AD 43 had been one such aristocratic boy, once he had completed his education and served his stint in the army, he might well have been established as a puppet or client king by the Roman authorities. This was not an uncommon practice in areas where the local people and their ruler were well-disposed towards Rome: the ruler would pay tax or tribute and, in return, would retain his status and estates under the protection of Rome. A 'police force' of Roman soldiers stationed in a small fort close to the chieftain's estate could underline the Roman support.

The Earliest Roman Town at Verulamium

A client kingdom in this part of south-east England was probably never intended to be more than a short-term arrangement. The chieftain's burial dates from about AD 55, and there is no evidence to suggest that the arrangement continued after his death. By the late 50s Verulamium was taking its first steps towards becoming a Roman town.

Whoever was the guiding force behind the establishment of Roman Verulamium, he apparently had fairly grandiose ideas – even at this early date the town had one, and quite possibly two,

masonry buildings. In the mid-first century, the area that was to become the centre of the Roman town was occupied by the ditched Central Enclosure, under what is now St Michael's churchyard. The enclosure ditch had not been filled in, and excavations within the enclosure in the early 1900s revealed masonry remains that clearly pre-dated the Roman Forum-Basilica complex completed in AD 79. Only short stretches of two walls together with small areas of mortar floors were uncovered in these early excavations, so we have no real idea as to the plan of the building. It could have been part of an early predecessor of the Forum, but it is possible that it derives from the 'palace' of the ruling family. Nevertheless, the presence of such remains is itself evidence of the importance of Verulamium at this date.

Rather firmer evidence was found in 1975, during excavations in advance of a pub extension 200 metres north of the 1900s excavation. Here part of a masonry bathhouse dating from about AD 50 was uncovered. The bathhouse included a cold plunge bath and was embellished with painted wall plaster with decorative motifs, among them a stylised lyre. The bath presumably used water from

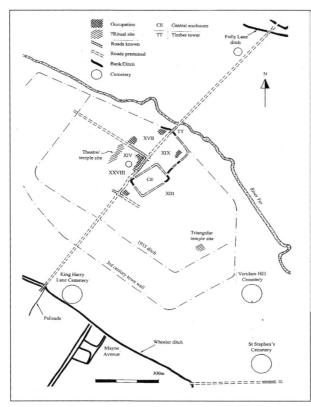

Fig. 3.7
Verulamium at about the time of the Boudican revolt in AD 60/61.
The town was comparatively small at this date, and was focused upon the Central Enclosure and its annex. By the end of the first century the town had almost doubled in size to the line of the 1955 ditch. By the third century the town walls enclosed over 200 acres.

the nearby river, and its presence here by the middle of the first century indicates that construction of the amenities of town life was in full swing. This implies that water-supply and drainage schemes were already in place.

The ditch defining the 'annex' on the north of the Central Enclosure was also still open. West of this was an area later occupied by the Roman theatre and temple, though it may already have been venerated as a sacred site in the pre-Roman period. On the other side of the river the ceremonial site surrounding the royal burial must have dominated the skyline and was probably already venerated as a shrine.

It is still not certain how far the layout of the earliest Roman town was influenced by existing occupation, especially round the area of the Central Enclosure.

Like all major Romano-British towns, from its earliest years

Roman Verulamium was divided into blocks, or *insulae*, by a grid of streets crossing one another at right angles. Some of these streets were probably already in existence before the Roman conquest but, as the town expanded, so the area covered by the street grid was extended. West of the Central Enclosure, in *insula* 14 of the later Roman town, a block of timber-framed workshops was erected shortly after the conquest. This was in an area that may already have been an 'industrial quarter' before the conquest, as fragments of clay moulds for casting coin blanks have been found nearby.

The early Roman building consisted of a row of workshops opening onto Watling Street through a covered portico or veranda. The entire block made up of seven different shops or workshops had been built as a single unit, presumably by a landowner or a speculator, who then rented out the shops or manned them with slaves or freedmen running them on his behalf. Most of the shops were concerned with various forms of metalworking although one seems to have sold samian pottery – glossy red tableware imported from southern France. The living quarters of the craftsmen were either on the first floor or behind the workshops (fig. 3.7).

AD 60: The Boudican Revolt and its Aftermath

The developing town came to grief in AD 60 during the revolt of Boudica. At the time of the conquest the Iceni of Norfolk and north Suffolk had formed a client kingdom similar to that suggested for the local Catuvellauni. The Icenian client king, Prasutagus, survived longer than his counterpart at Verulamium, dying shortly before AD 60. The subsequent incorporation of his kingdom into the Roman province, however, far from proceeding smoothly – as was apparently the case at Verulamium – culminated in the outbreak of a serious revolt, led by Prasutagus' widow, Boudica.

The Iceni were joined by the neighbouring Trinovantes of Essex, who were smarting under a number of grievances, not least the loss of land that had been granted to veteran Roman soldiers. Taking advantage of the fact that the bulk of the Roman army was away campaigning in north Wales, the rebels burnt both Colchester and London to the ground and slaughtered the inhabitants. They then pressed on to Verulamium, where they meted out the same treatment. Layers of burnt clay and charcoal have been found, masking the remains of the workshops in *insula* 14. No site in the town that was occupied in the 50s escaped destruction in AD 60.

It is not difficult to understand the rebels' motives in attacking Verulamium. Not long before, the local ruler had probably thrown in his lot with Rome, and, on his death, his followers had been quite prepared to acquiesce in Roman rule. They were now enthusiastically building themselves a Roman town. Clearly the rebels saw the emerging town as nothing more than a nest of collaborators, on whom they wreaked their revenge at the first opportunity.

Verulamium in the Later First and Second Centuries

There was no overnight recovery after the Boudican destruction. Although some survivors may have returned to pick up the pieces, several sites in the town remained vacant for about 15 years. It was not until the last quarter of the first century that Verulamium's fortunes really revived, and this resurgence may well have been result of a deliberate policy of romanisation instigated by the Roman authorities. The Roman historian, Tacitus, gave the credit for this policy to his father-in-law, Agricola, who was governor of Britain between AD 79 and 85. Certainly it was during Agricola's governorship that the Verulamium Basilica was completed, as his name appears on the dedicatory inscription put up in the autumn of 79.

The Basilica, with the Forum to the south of it, together made up an imposing complex in the centre of the late first-century town and on the site of the earlier Central Enclosure. Today the whole Forum-Basilica complex lies buried deep beneath the church and vicarage of St Michael's. Small-scale excavations over the years have allowed the overall plan to be reconstructed, but details of the buildings remain unknown. The Basilica consisted of a massive hall over 120 metres long; with an estimated height of 30 metres, it must have towered over the surrounding buildings.

On either side of the central hall was a row of small offices, and the hall itself was divided into aisles by

31

arcades of limestone columns. The Basilica would have housed the shrine of the local god as well as the law courts. Here legal disputes would have been resolved and magistrates would have pontificated on non-capital charges.

On the south-west side of the Basilica was the Forum. This consisted of a large colonnaded courtyard. On the east and west sides of the courtyard, small rooms or offices opened off the colonnades. These would have been used as shops, schoolrooms and stores to house census records and tax returns. The Forum was the commercial and financial centre of the town, and it was here that taxation records of the community would have been kept.

In the centre of the south colonnade, opposite the Basilica, was a classical temple, no doubt dedicated to the emperor and the state gods of Rome. This would have been used for official events – for instance, for religious ceremonies observed on the Emperor's birthday and other state occasions. In the later second century another classical temple was added at the west corner of the Forum. A third building, at the south corner of the Forum, may also have been a temple, although an interpretation as a *curia* – the meeting place of the town council – is a more likely alternative. As the only large Roman town known from the territory of the Catuvellauni, Verulamium was almost certainly the tribal capital during the Roman period. Consequently it was here where tribal matters would have been decided.

In spite of its enormous size, the completion of the Forum-Basilica complex was only one element in a carefully designed scheme for the rebuilding of Verulamium. The late first-century town was planned to cover an area of 100 acres (40 hectares), similar to that of the *colonia* at Colchester, which at the time of the Boudican revolt was the principal town in the province. By the time Tacitus was writing in the early second century AD, Verulamium enjoyed the status of a *municipium*. This meant that the town would have had a carefully drawn-up charter laying down detailed and specific regulations. Within these rules, however, Verulamium may have enjoyed a certain degree of autonomy. It is not at all certain when Verulamium first became a

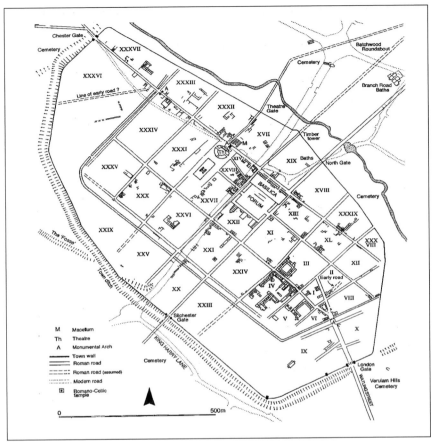

Fig. 3.8 Verulamium, showing the street grid, the principal buildings and the insulae.

municipium, but it was probably in the 70s and 80s of the first century when the town was rapidly expanding (fig. 3.8).

The task of building the Forum and Basilica must have been an enormous one, but it was not the only major public building put up in the town during the late first century. The best known of these is the *macellum*, or market hall, which covered a total area of 880 square metres, and consisted of eighteen small rooms opening onto a central courtyard. A narrow gateway led onto Watling Street. The plan is very like those of *macella* and warehouses in Roman towns on the continent. The large quantity of animal bones that have been found in this area

33

suggests it may have been the meat market.

Several temples with flint and masonry foundations were also completed at about this time. At the southern entrance to the first-century town, the triangular temple, so called because of the unusual plan of its *temenus* or precinct, was completed in about AD 85, while west of the Forum a large temple was built in *insula* 16, on a site that may possibly already have been sacred before the conquest. Three other temples are known from Verulamium, but their dates have not been established.

With the exception of the Forum temples, which were classical in design, all the Verulamium temples were of the so-called Romano-Celtic type, characterised by a square or rectangular shrine housing the cult figure, surrounded by a veranda or portico where offerings could be displayed.

It is likely that the public baths were built now. The mid-first-century baths had been patched up after the Boudican revolt and were used for several years. By the end of the century, however, they were abandoned, presumably because new, and perhaps even grander, baths were now available. In 1988 two masonry vaulted drains,

apparently dating from the late first or early second centuries, were found in *insula* 3, a short distance south-east of the Forum. Dating evidence was very sparse and the excavation itself was very restricted, but the massive character of drains suggests the presence of baths, probably public ones.

One hundred and twenty five metres north-west of the Forum, on the opposite side of Watling Street to the *macellum* and close to the *insula* 16 temple, was the Verulamium theatre. This was built in about AD 140 on a site that had previously been kept clear of buildings. It is difficult to escape the conclusion that the site had been specially reserved as a theatre site from the first century. Although theatres are known or suspected from other Romano-British towns, the Verulamium theatre is the only one that can be visited today.

Several Roman towns had amphitheatres – oval-shaped areas surrounded by earth banks. Amphitheatres, however, lack the stage, changing room and apparatus for raising and lowering the curtain in front of the stage. These were needed for dramatic performances and are found in the

Verulamium theatre, but were not required for the types of entertainment provided in amphitheatres.

Public buildings apart, the generation after the Boudican revolt would have seen an astonishing expansion of the town, from an area of about 10 hectares in AD 60 to 40 hectares in the 80s. By the end of the century shops and houses were spreading along the streets. The street grid had been replaced and extended after the fire and gradually shops and houses were built along them.

When the town was first defended is a question that has still to be resolved. At some stage in the first century a ditch was dug round three sides of the town. The ditch, known as the 1955 Ditch after the year in which it was first recognised, was a substantial one – up to 3.5 metres deep and up to 6.7 metres wide at the mouth with a steep V-shaped profile. Originally there was a corresponding earth bank probably on its inner side.

The 1955 Ditch never existed along the north-east side of the town, nearest the river, presumably because the un-drained valley floor gave sufficient protection on this side. It is

possible that the 1955 Ditch defended the original pre-Boudican town, but recent research suggests it was not dug until the expansion of the town in the last quarter of the century.

One of the most eloquent discoveries in recent years must be the recovery, on a building site, of a burial dating from about AD

Fig. 3.9 Grave offerings from a burial just outside Verulamium and dating from approximately AD 85.
The cremated ashes of the dead were contained in the large glass jar (to the right). The offerings include iron strigils, (used in Roman bath suites) black and white gaming counters (bottom right), four lamps, the iron frame for a folding stool (top left), a bronze bowl and a 13 piece dinner service made in samian ware imported from southern France.

85. The cremated ashes of the dead person were contained in a magnificent glass jar and accompanied by a large collection of imported samian tableware, a fine bronze owl of continental workmanship, oil lamps, gaming counters, strigils and a remarkable iron tripod, possibly the frame for a folding stool (fig. 3.9). This burial must have been deposited at much the same time as Tacitus was commenting that the Britons were adopting a taste for dinner parties, luxurious bath suites, and romanised fashions.

The late first and early second centuries saw the beginnings of a period of prosperity for the town. Iron-working continued in the area around Berkhamsted, and in Verulamium itself numerous smithies flourished throughout this time. The workshops north-west of the Forum-Basilica complex, which had been burnt to the ground in the Boudican revolt, were rebuilt some thirty years later on lines almost identical to those of their predecessors. Soon afterwards further shops sprang up to the west of them. Metalworking, baking, brewing and leather-working are all attested.

East of the Forum-Basilica granaries and large hearths were almost certainly used by brewers to produce the British beer which, by the end of the third century, was sufficiently well-known to merit inclusion in the Emperor Diocletian's price fixing edicts.

Elsewhere there is evidence for leather and bone working, as well as for fine metalworking. For the most part these industries took place in modest workshops opening onto the street, with living premises behind. It is remarkable that nearly all the private houses found in the town at this date show signs of some sort of industry or craft being practised in them. The sounds of metalworking, the smoke from dozens of furnaces and kilns, and the stench of leather-tanning must have permeated the town.

The local pottery industry operated on a much larger scale. Kilns were first established 5 kilometres south of Verulamium in about AD 50, and were probably run by immigrant potters from Gaul. The Boudican revolt does not seem to have caused any lasting setback to the industry, which flourished for at least a hundred years. By the early second century tile and pottery kilns occupied a broad but discontinuous band along Watling Street from Verulamium to Brockley Hill, just outside Elstree.

Fig. 3.10 Leather off-cuts from a late first-century rubbish dump and an iron wool-carding comb from the Gorhambury villa.

Although supplying local demand, the bulk of the pottery was exported: by the first half of the second century products of the Verulamium kilns were flooding into the London market. It is possible that the kiln products were shipped by barge down the Colne to the Thames at Staines. Remains of a wooden wharf were excavated in 1954 on the bank of the Ver at Park Street, 4.5 kilometres south-east of Verulamium and close to several kiln sites (fig. 3.10).

In spite of all this evidence for industry Verulamium must have been primarily a market town, serving its rural hinterland and dependent on it. Land close to

Verulamium was probably farmed by the townspeople themselves. Even inside the town itself, large areas were not built up and appear to have been used as market gardens or orchards. Areas of dark earth with a high humus content probably represent cultivated plots – gardens, paddocks, orchards or smallholdings. These have been found over quite wide areas near the town centre in the early second century, and, although the street frontages were built up, the centre of the *insulae* often remained open. A significant number of agricultural tools have been found in Verulamium, underlining the importance of market gardening and agriculture to the inhabitants (fig. 3.11).

Much can be learnt of the inhabitants themselves from the cemeteries that surrounded Verulamium. A strictly observed law forbade the burial of anyone over the age of forty days within the

Fig. 3.11 A collection of iron tips for ploughshares. All were found in Verulamium and underline the importance of agriculture to the town's inhabitants.

37

town, and so, as at all other Roman towns, extensive cemeteries grew up immediately outside.

The main cemetery in use in the late first and second centuries lay on the crest of St Stephen's hill, half a kilometre south of the town. Here nearly 400 burials have been excavated since the last century, most of them dating from between about AD 60 and 200. During this period the predominant burial rite was cremation, which limits the survival of information on the age, health and sex of the dead person. Nevertheless, a study of these graves leads to the conclusion that, on the whole, the inhabitants of Roman Verulamium could enjoy a reasonable life expectancy, were not unduly prone to illness, dietary deficiencies or accidents, and led robust, if rather hard, lives.

Their grave offerings are not particularly remarkable, but suggest reasonable affluence: these people must have been the housewives and tradesmen of the town, who were buried in small groups on either side of Watling Street, overlooking a town where they had spent their lives. Successful merchants based in Verulamium no doubt commissioned expensive monuments that would have flanked the main roads leading out of the town. For many years a large block of carved limestone lay half submerged in the River Ver, before being recognised as part of an elaborate 'tower' tomb of a type used by rich merchants in London and Trier.

The leading members of society were buried elsewhere. Rich landowners were probably buried on their country estates, perhaps in an elaborate mausoleum like that excavated in 1936-7 at Rothamsted, 6 kilometres upstream from Verulamium, or more recently at Wood Lane End, Hemel Hempstead. Two exceptionally rich burials, both dating from the second century, have recently been found on what is probably the site of a villa, some 8 kilometres north of Verulamium between Harpenden and Wheathampstead. The cremated ashes of the dead were accompanied by magnificent glass and bronze vessels including jugs, dishes and bowls, many of which must have been imported from Italy. Hunting equipment in one grave underlines the aristocratic pursuits of these romanised descendants of the old tribal aristocracy, still living on their ancestral estates.

Throughout the early years of the second century private houses were built of timber. Sleeper beams supported timber frames, infilled with wattle and daub and coated with lime plaster. Roofs were generally tiled, and the floors either of mortar or beaten clay, though some were planked. Until about AD 140 only temples or public buildings had masonry walls, but by the middle of the second century some house-holders were starting to rebuild their properties – giving them flint and mortar foundations.

It was a time when the citizens of Verulamium were taking pride in their houses and spending money on them. The earliest mosaic and tessellated floors in Verulamium were laid now, and for the first time painted frescoes appeared on the walls of the dining and reception rooms of the well-to-do – a form of interior decoration that villa owners in the surrounding countryside had been enjoying for at least a generation.

All this was brought to a halt by a second fire, which broke out sometime between about AD 155 and 170 and which destroyed a large part of Verulamium. The wooden construction of most of the homes no doubt encouraged the spread of the fire, which totally destroyed about two-thirds of the town. Even the stone-built Forum-Basilica complex was completely destroyed.

Chapter 4
Verulamium in its Heyday: AD 200–350
Rosalind Niblett

The mid-second-century fire must have dealt a disastrous blow to many of the townspeople. The Forum-Basilica complex was rebuilt, but the cost must have put an enormous financial burden on a town crippled by the destruction of many of the businesses and workshops that had previously lined its streets. It is hardly surprising that some city-centre sites lay empty for up to 50 years after the fire. Nevertheless the town gradually recovered and, in spite of the political instability and inflation that hit much of the Roman Empire, the late second and early third centuries seem to have been a time of prosperity for Verulamium.

At the end of the second century the masonry drains in *insula* 3 were replaced by a building with still more massive masonry foundations, a splendid vaulted drain and a hypocaust. All this reinforces the interpretation of the site as that of the main public baths. Cleanliness and hygiene had become important concerns to the inhabitants of Verulamium. Early in the third century one enterprising shop owner, whose premises occupied a prime site between the Forum and the theatre, operated a large public lavatory, flushed by piped water and draining into one of the town's four brick-built sewers. By the third and fourth centuries several large houses included their own private bath suites. Clearly there was no shortage of running water in Verulamium. The inhabitants of the lower-lying areas of the town had a piped water supply distributed through wooden pipes as early as the early second century, if not before, while a new pipe bringing water to the centre of the town was laid as late as the fifth century. A timber-lined leat or aqueduct seems to have brought water to the town from the Ver, tapping the river further upstream, close to the modern village of Redbourn.

Towards the end of the second century the Verulamium theatre was rebuilt. Like many other provincial theatres, when it was first built the Verulamium example had a comparatively small stage but a correspondingly large orchestra – the flat, arena-like area in the centre of horseshoe arrangement of seats that forms the *cavea*, or auditorium. When the theatre was first built the orchestra, rather than the stage, was the main focus of attention. Later on the orchestra was reduced in size and the stage extended and elaborated, presumably reflecting an increased interest in theatrical performances rather than displays of wrestling or bear-baiting more suited to the arena-like orchestra. Nevertheless, throughout its life the prime use of the theatre was not simply to provide the inhabitants of Verulamium with entertainment, but to accommodate worshippers during religious rites, when plays were performed as part of religious festivals.

The Verulamium theatre was associated with two temples linked by a road: one stood immediately behind the theatre in *insula* 16, and the other stood on the opposite side of the river on the ceremonial site that was centred on the first-century chieftain's burial at Folly Lane (described in Chapter 3). Here a substantial temple stood directly over the site of the chieftain's funeral pyre, and faced towards his grave. Slightly down hill from the Folly Lane temple a large bathhouse had been built in about AD 140. This faced way from the town and towards the Folly Lane temple, and was clearly associated with it. It was probably used by cult followers in purification rituals prior to attending the Folly Lane temple.

The area between the baths and temple was riddled with deep pits, some containing deposits suggesting that they served a ritual function and that votive deposits were placed in them. One third-century pit contained the severed head of a young man who had been killed by a blow on the head and had than been scalped. The whole complex, temple, burial site, pits and baths, was linked by a specially built road or processional way, leading to the Verulamium theatre and the *insula* 16 temple behind it. It is difficult to escape the conclusion that by the later second century the site of the first-century chieftain's burial had become the focus for an important tribal cult.

The severed head in the Folly Lane pit hints at bizarre rituals, but it was far from being the only cult observed in the town. As the Roman period progressed, there is

Fig. 4.1 Mithras, the Persian god of light, as depicted on a late second-century beaker found in Verulamium.

increasing evidence from the town for a variety of religious cults: Cybele, the Near-Eastern Earth Mother, was probably worshipped in the triangular temple; Serapis, the Egyptian god of rebirth, is depicted on a gemstone from a finger ring; and Mithras, the Persian god of light, is shown on a bronze 'token' found in the rubble of what was once a comfortable town house. Numerous fragments of small statues represent the Graeco-Roman deities Mercury, Minerva, Hercules, Venus and Bacchus. The quality of two of them, Venus and Mercury, is as high as any from Roman Britain, as is the standard of workmanship of many of the gemstones (figs. 4.1 and 4.2).

This sophistication is reflected in the houses built by the more prosperous inhabitants of the town. Many houses were now provided with flint and mortar footings, even though the superstructures were often still of wood and plaster. The character of many of the buildings themselves changed. Although workshops were rebuilt on some street frontages, elsewhere we find just two later buildings on a site that previously was occupied by several smaller shops or houses. By the end of the century houses with up to 15 rooms on the ground floor alone were being constructed, and what appear to be stairwells in several houses suggest that

Fig 4.2 Bronze statuette of Mercury accompanied by his traditional attributes – a ram, a cock and a tortoise. Mercury is wearing a tiny silver torc around his neck. Found immediately south of the third-century town wall.

Fig. 4.3 Sir Mortimer Wheeler excavating the shell mosaic in 1930.

upper floors were not uncommon. The rooms were often arranged on two or three sides of a courtyard or garden, facing south-east, although courtyards with ranges of rooms on all four sides were always a rarity in Verulamium.

Houses now began to show signs of considerable refinement, and the post-fire period saw the widespread use of tessellated and mosaic floors. Remains of more than 30 mosaics have been recorded over the years, and of these roughly two-thirds date from the period AD 150–220.

Mosaics with human or animal figures are rare in Verulamium. Fragments of a lively hunting scene survive from a floor behind a third-century shop in *insula* 14, and the well-preserved mosaic from a large house in *insula* 21,

showing a lion carrying a stag's head in its mouth, dates from about AD 180. The head of a god is shown on a late second-century mosaic from *insula* 8; whether the god is Sylvanus or Neptune depends on whether the projections from his head are interpreted as horns or lobster claws. Purely geometric designs are far commoner, and the shell mosaic from *insula* 2 provides a superb example. This floor lay in a semicircular apse, opening from a large room which contained a second mosaic and which may have been a dining room (fig. 4.3).

Wall-painting now reached its peak, with elaborate designs painted on both walls and ceilings. One of the most attractive examples is the frieze that occupied the top of the

43

Fig. 4.4 Painted wall plaster from a mid-second-century house.

corridor wall outside the room with the lion mosaic in *insula* 21. Here a series of pheasants is shown, perched within the flowing tendrils of a vine. This wall plaster is now on display in the British Museum. Generally, however, the Verulamium wall paintings imitated architectural features, particularly columns, and were painted to resemble marble. They were all true frescoes in that the paint was applied to wet plaster, and originally must have been extremely bright and, to modern eyes, somewhat overwhelming in their impact (fig. 4.4).

The evidence for widespread industrial activity seen in the Verulamium of the later first and early second centuries is not immediately apparent in the later town, but this does not mean that industry did not continue to play an important part in the town's life.

The local pottery industry declined in the later second century, although it continued to produce cooking pots and storage jars for a purely local market for at least another century. Many of the large third- and fourth-century houses in Verulamium included ranges of small, rather box-like rooms that were probably used as stores or workshops. What trades or crafts were practised in these establishments is less certain.

A large house in *insula* 5, excavated in the 1930s, contained concrete-lined tanks up to 5 by 4 metres and over a metre deep. It is possible that these were installed by people concerned with cloth-processing such as fulling or dyeing. Rather similar tanks from Roman sites in France have been interpreted in this way. There is some evidence that wool production played an important economic role in the Catuvellaunian territory in the Roman period. A wool-carding comb was found in a third-century rubbish pit at the nearby villa at Gorhambury, and two more examples were found in the early 1990s in late Roman pits just outside the town.

Agriculture also continued to play an important part in the economic life of Verulamium, and several barns and ovens for processing corn are known within or just outside the city. The ovens could also have been used for malting grain from brewing, and the Verulamium breweries no doubt continued to thrive.

The large areas of open ground surrounding many of the buildings speak of the continued importance of market gardening and smal-lholdings, but do not necessarily mean a reduction in population. It is quite conceivable that small-scale enterprises, both inside and outside the town boundaries, were unable either to recover from the late second-century fire or to cope with the high taxation and inflation of the third century. It is possible that in many cases these small business and livelihoods were swallowed up by more successful concerns, and that by the fourth century many families who had once worked in small workshops on the street frontages were now housed in the service wings or upper floors of the large houses of their wealthier neighbours.

The population of Verulamium at this or any other period is almost impossible to estimate. In the past it has been suggested that up to 20,000 people may have lived here. It is becoming clear, however, that the town was never densely built up, and probably the population was considerably less than this; it may never have much exceeded 5,000.

Verulamium has suffered badly over the centuries both from the depredations of medieval builders, who dug out the flint and tile in the footings of many Roman buildings for reuse in the Abbey, and through natural erosion of the valley slope. As a result a vast quantity of information on the life of the town has been lost, particularly that

Fig. 4.5 Fragment from a woollen cloak or blanket from a third-century child's grave.

relating to the third and fourth centuries.

There is no reason to suppose, however, that in the later Roman period the leading citizens of Verulamium were not a prosperous and cultivated group of people. The medieval historian Matthew Paris recorded the discovery of scrolls in one Roman building in the town, although whether these were part of a private library or official town records in the Forum-Basilica is something we shall never know. We can be sure, however, that throughout the four centuries of Roman rule a host of merchants, businessmen, tax gatherers and officials continually brought new ideas and influences into the town from all quarters of the Roman Empire.

The surviving possessions of some of the townspeople, like the necklace of gilded glass beads from a second-century burial on St Stephen's hill or the bundle of gold thread from a third-century child's grave a short distance outside the London Gate, speak of people who appreciated fine things and had the wherewithal to acquire them (fig. 4.5).

At the same time the people of Roman Verulamium were ultimately of Catuvellaunian stock and no doubt retained much of their native culture. This is partly demonstrated by the popularity of designs incorporating flowing curvilinear lines, which are a characteristic of pre-Roman art (fig. 4.6).

Fig. 4.6. A 'hunt cup' decorated with hares and hounds – third century.

Matthew Paris tells us that one at least of the scrolls found by the early medieval monks in the Roman town was written in the 'British' language, and although official business would have been conducted in Latin, Celtic must have been used in most conversations in Verulamium.

Many of the tribal gods continued to be worshipped in the Roman period. The so-called 'mother goddess' clay figurines of Venus are typical of the north-western provinces of the empire, and several have been found in Verulamium, while the growth of the religious complex on the site of the first-century chieftain's burial is sufficient testimony to the persistence of native cults.

By the third century the earlier rite of cremation burial was giving way to that of inhumation. This may have been partly due to fashion and partly due to the growth of religions preaching the resurrection of the body, among them Christianity. Late Roman inhumation cemeteries spread round the north side of the town, occupying areas once marshy but drained when the Ver was canalised in the third century. Inhumation means that more information survives about the

Fig. 4.7 *The face of a wealthy third-century citizen of Verulamium. Reconstructed by Richard Neave from the remarkably well-preserved skeleton buried in a lead coffin.*

physical appearance of the townspeople, allowing the face of one third-century man to be reconstructed using modern forensic techniques (fig. 4.7).

The Town Walls, Gateways and Monumental Arches

By the third century the old earth defence, the 1955 Ditch, had long since been filled in, and the town had expanded beyond it. At some stage, work had started on a second earthwork defence represented today by the Fosse earthwork on the south-west of the town. The exact course of the Fosse is still uncertain, and it may never have been completed. At all events, at some point in the third century work started on the town wall.

The wall was over 3 metres thick at the foundation level, although only just over 2 metres thick further up. It was faced with squared flint nodules, and the core between the two faces was filled with flint rubble and mortar. Today, the original facing has long gone, and all that is visible in the surviving stretches is the core. The town walls formed a complete circuit round Verulamium, with a total length of 3.6 kilometres, enclosing an area of 81 hectares, or 203 acres. This made Verulamium the third largest walled town in Britain, only exceeded by Cirencester and London. The original height of the walls is unknown, but it was probably nearly 4 metres to the parapet. The greatest surviving height is nearly 3 metres.

Small wall towers with projecting semicircular bastions were built at the same time as the wall on the southern side. Bastions were used to mount catapults to provide extra defence, although there is no sign that Verulamium's walls were built at a time of danger, nor is it easy to

Fig. 4.8 The third-century town walls.
The projecting flint and mortar footing in the foreground is the south wall of one of the drum towers that flanked the London Gateway on the south side of the town.

see how so large a walled circuit could be effectively defended by the inhabitants.

As the wall was being built, a deep ditch was dug in front of it, and the material piled up behind the wall to provide a bank giving easy access to the wall parapet. Large gateways marked the four main entrances to the town, towering above the level of the town wall itself. All four gates were massive structures with double carriage-ways and flanking pedestrian passageways. In addition there was a small postern gate on the north side of the town, through which the road connecting the theatre with the royal burial site passed (fig. 4.8).

Verulamium was unusual in possessing three monumental arches, which served a symbolic rather than a practical purpose. Two were put up at the points at which Watling Street crossed the late first-century earthwork defence. They date from the third century and were built to mark the boundaries of the late first-century town at a time when the original earthwork defence had been long since obliterated. Only the flint and mortar foundations survive, but these arches must have been massive structures, similar to

monumental arches known from the Continent. Originally they were faced with dressed stone, and no doubt embellished with inscriptions and sculpture, but nothing of these have survived.The third arch, which must have been similar in style, was built early in the fourth century. It linked the theatre with the *macellum* opposite it.

Verulamium in the Fifth and Sixth Centuries

The prosperity evident in Verulamium in the early third century seems to have continued through the fourth century. In the surrounding countryside, however, many villas started to decline in the course of the third century, and it is possible that the political and economic instability of the times encouraged some villa owners to move their families to the town, leaving stewards to run their country estates. Several large barns and corn-drying ovens are known within or close to the town; it may be that in the late Roman period landowners found it was no longer advisable to store and process harvested grain away from the safety of the town.

It has already been suggested that as the Roman period advanced there was a tendency for small enterprises to be swallowed up by large establishments, and this trend may have intensified as time went on. Certainly the pattern of occupation in the southern part of Verulamium in the fourth century suggests that by that time there were fewer houses than in earlier centuries, but that these were very extensive and presumably housed larger numbers of people.

There is some evidence that a further fire destroyed part of the central area of Verulamium in the early fourth century. The baths in *insula* 3, rebuilt in the early third century, seem to have been demolished in the early fourth and may never have been rebuilt. Across the street from the baths, a house in the south corner of *insula* 13 was burnt down at about the same time, although here re-building took place quickly. The *macellum* in *insula* 17 was also rebuilt in the early fourth century and provided with a monumental facade along Watling Street.

There is no doubt that sufficient wealth was still available for large private houses to be kept in reasonable repair and even extended. As late as about AD 390 repairs were being carried out to the mosaic floor in the

magnificent reception room of a house close to the Forum in *insula* 27, and at much the same time the open area in front of the Basilica was resurfaced. Drains and street surfaces in the area east of the Forum also continued to be maintained. Right at the end of the fourth century the *insula* 16 temple on the south side of the theatre was repaired, although by this time both the theatre and the temple associated with the chieftain's burial site on the other side of the river had fallen into disuse.

By the fifth century Verulamium had become an established Christian centre, probably attracting pilgrims from further afield. Two buildings excavated in or just outside the Roman town have been tentatively identified as churches. The focus of late Roman Christianity in Verulamium, however, lay a short distance outside the town at the shrine of St Alban.

St Alban was an inhabitant of Verulamium who was probably martyred at some point in the third century. The precise date of this is unknown. It has been argued that the martyrdom took place during the reign of the Emperor Septimus Severus (198–211), but this view has now been challenged in favour of a rather later date, perhaps during the reigns of Decius (249–251) or Valerian (257–259), when persecutions of Christians are known to have taken place. In fact the precise date will probably never be established to everyone's satisfaction.

According to the earliest account that has come down to us, St Alban was executed on a hill, 500 paces outside Verulamium and on the other side of a river. The geography of Verulamium fits this description quite well, and supports the theory that the medieval abbey is either close to or actually over the site of the martyr's grave. Excavations in the 1980s failed to find the martyr's grave but did reveal a third-century cemetery on the south side of the medieval abbey. It now seems likely the grave lay somewhere in this cemetery, the full extent of which is still not clear.

Early in the fifth century the last remnants of the Roman army were withdrawn from Britain, never to return. In AD 410 Britain effectively ceased to be part of the Roman Empire with the Emperor Honorius' instruction to the province to arrange its own defence against barbarian raids. After the early fifth

century the fate of Verulamium, along with that of other Romano-British towns, is very obscure, although evidence is gradually accumulating to suggest that the people of Verulamium continued to enjoy their prosperity for several decades.

In AD 429 St Germanus, Bishop of Auxerre, visited Britain to combat a heretical movement that was attracting a large number of adherents and threatening to split the British Church. After successfully confronting the heretics, Germanus proceeded to Verulamium, where he paid his respects at St Alban's shrine. Although his next engagement was the routing of an army of Saxon raiders, there is nothing in his chronicler's account to suggest that this definitely took place in the vicinity of Verulamium, and there is no indication in the archaeological record of the presence of Saxons in the local area at this date.

Although a third-century house in *insula* 27 was demolished at some point in the early fifth century it was replaced by a large, masonry barn or hall with solidly built flint and mortar foundations supported by sturdy wooden piles in places where it overlay earlier

51

pits. Furthermore, it is clear that at least some of the town's amenities were still being maintained even later. A timber water pipe, supplying the town centre with fresh water, was subsequently inserted through the foundations of the barn. While we cannot tell the precise date of either the barn or the water pipe, they must date from well within the fifth century.

There is no doubt, however, that gradually various skills and crafts ceased to be practised, and Verulamium slowly decayed. With the departure of the army, new coinage, once brought in to pay the troops, ceased to reach Britain in any quantity. This in turn led to the disappearance of a coin-based economy and the growth of barter. Trade declined as travelling became more difficult. The main road from Verulamium to Colchester seems to have been falling into disrepair as early as the late third century, and, as the menace of raids grew (whether by Saxon marauders or disaffected peasants), so trade must have dwindled still further. As a result, established industries died. The pottery industry was one of the first, with ceramic pots presumably being replaced by vessels of wood and metal.

With the disappearance of pottery and coins the archaeologist's task of dating the latest phases of the Roman town becomes very difficult. In fact the latest buildings in Verulamium are virtually without pottery, and they appear to belong to a time when the flint and mortar houses of the third and fourth centuries had been replaced by less elaborate houses built entirely in wood. In two cases

Fig. 4.9 Post holes outlining an early post-Roman wooden building outside the north-east gate of Verulamium.

simple wooden buildings were built on the surfaces of earlier town streets, where the gravel metalling offered well-drained level surfaces, no doubt relatively free of debris from crumbling masonry buildings (fig. 4.9).

These wooden buildings have been identified on three separate sites within the town and may well date from as late as the sixth century. Certainly four very similar buildings have been excavated recently, short distances outside the town. Three stood on the gravel surface of the Colchester road as it crossed the now deserted site at Folly Lane, and the fourth stood beside Watling Street as it ran through the abandoned Roman cemetery on St Stephen's Hill. These wooden buildings were simple rectangular single-roomed houses, solidly constructed with substantial timber posts. The three on the Folly Lane site fronted onto a muddy track that snaked its way up the hillside from the river crossing at Kingsbury. Lying in the mud that accumulated on this track were sherds of crude handmade pottery, liberally tempered with chaff and dating to the sixth century or later.

Although at no point is there any evidence for a violent end to Verulamium, these buildings are a far cry from the sophisticated houses of the Roman town. A century later a group of Saxon settlers was buried on the opposite side of the river, and the transition from provincial Roman town to Anglo-Saxon village must have been complete.

Chapter 5

Farming the Roman Chilterns

Keith Branigan

It is ironic that the one estate of which we have firm evidence, and even the owner's name (Sullonius), should be an industrial estate rather than a farm. The greater part of the Chilterns was undoubtedly held by landowning farmers who looked to Verulamium for both their social and their economic focus.

They lived mostly on villa estates spread down the valleys of the dip-slope. In the western Chilterns the villas are quite evenly spread down the valleys, and we can estimate that their estates included perhaps 500–600 acres (200-240 hectares) of arable and pasture in addition to extensive tracts of woodland. There were about 40 such villa estates in this area, with a small number to the east of Verulamium and seven or eight strung along the foot of the scarp (fig. 5.1).

Several of the villa buildings are known to have been erected over pre-Roman farmhouses, and it is likely that many of the villa estates were based on late Iron Age land holdings by members of the tribal aristocracy. The villas at Gorhambury, Park Street and Lockleys are good examples of this suspected continuity.

The extent to which continuity of ownership saw the retention of traditional native ways of farming is still debated, but we should certainly not expect rapid change in the farming regimes or methods following the Roman invasion. The innate conservatism of farmers and constraints of soils and topography were sufficient to ensure that changes would be slow and gradual.

The Chilterns are natural 'mixed' farming country with a variety of soils, flora and fauna. The hill tops and slopes are covered by clay with flints, and the valley floors with alluvium, but there are many patches of other materials, such as clayey chalk marl, pebbly glacial drifts and reddish brick earth.

The woodlands that covered the hill tops and spread down the slopes were themselves mixed, with oak, elm, birch, ash, alder, poplar and, by this time, considerable numbers of beech.

54

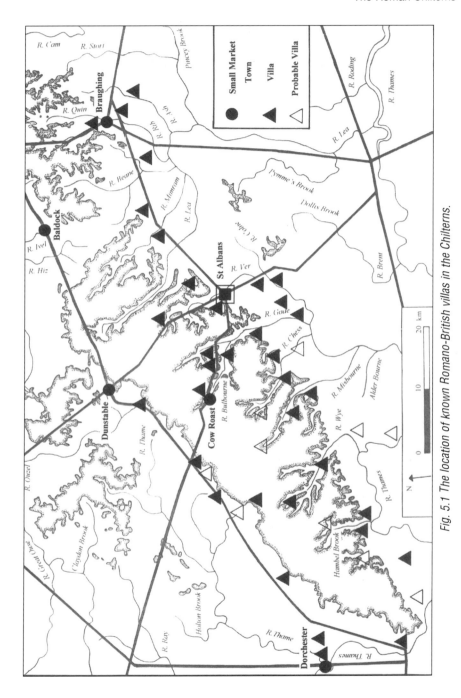

Fig. 5.1 The location of known Romano-British villas in the Chilterns.

Within the woodlands ran red, fallow and roe deer, wild boar and a variety of smaller animals. Other wild food sources included pigeon and woodcock, and trout and roach in the rivers. In medieval and early modern times this attractive and varied environment has been exploited by farmers for both mixed stock-raising and arable farming, and this was probably true in the Roman period.

The best arable land, for drainage as well as soils, lay on the slopes of the valleys, but sadly no convincing examples of Roman field systems survive in the Chilterns, unless small irregular fields at Ashridge prove Roman. The appearance of one-way plough marks at the Latimer and Gadebridge villas, however, and of a bar-share and coulter (ie blade mounted to cut the turf vertically) amongst farm tools found in Verulamium, suggest that longer, narrower fields may have replaced the traditional small roughly square 'Celtic' fields, perhaps by the beginning of the second century.

The adoption of one-way ploughing, as opposed to cross ploughing, and of longer fields meant more efficient ploughing in two respects. First, the same amount of land could be ploughed more quickly and, second, the same area of field produced more crops, because the only headlands were along the two narrow ends of the fields. If these new field systems were introduced, then it would have changed the appearance of the

Chiltern landscape quite dramatically.

The crops sown in these fields were mainly wheat and barley, the commonest form of wheat being spelt. The Chilterns produce wheat of good quality but rather low yield, and it may be that barley was as popular amongst the Roman farmers as wheat. If wheat was the winter-sown crop, as in the medieval period, then barley may have been sown in the spring. Whether the corn drying ovens found at Sarratt, Foxholes, Saunderton and elsewhere were used to parch the spelt before threshing, or rather in preparing barley for beer-making (fig. 5.2), is still debated, but in any event they provide welcome additional evidence for cereal production.

Harvesting and threshing were still labour-intensive activities in the Roman period. There is no evidence that the British farmers ever used the donkey-driven reaping machine known as the *vallus* and employed across the Channel in Gaul, and so crops would have been laboriously cut with small sickles like those found at Hambleden.

Similarly, milling of the corn into flour appears to have been done on hand-driven rotary querns rather than in donkey-powered or water-driven mills, for which there is a little evidence elsewhere in southern Britain. The querns used in the Chilterns villas were of two types. The rather flat stones, about 50 to 60 centimetres in diameter, were imported into the region from either the Pennines or the Rhineland and made from millstone grit or Nidermendig lava respectively. The smaller 'beehive' querns are a local product, however, made of the distinctive Hertfordshire puddingstone (fig. 5.3). Given the cost of transporting heavy products overland (even from London) to Verulamium, the Hertfordshire millstones must have had a competitive edge in the local market.

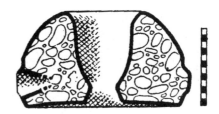

Fig. 5.3 A rotary millstone made of Hertfordshire puddingstone, found at Hunsdown.

It is noticeable that separate granary buildings are rarely found in the Chiltern villas; that at Gorhambury is the only clear example. Elsewhere, rooms set aside for grain storage have sometimes been identified in other buildings, but this suggests that large-scale storage of grain was not contemplated by the Chiltern farmers. We must conclude that once the farmers had taken enough for their own needs, most of the remainder was carted off immediately to market in Verulamium.

The absence of special grain storage facilities also suggests that the considerable numbers of pigs reared in the Chiltern farms were not grain-fed in sties, but were run by swineherds in the woodlands along the upper slopes and hill tops. The number of pigs represented in the samples of animal bone from Chiltern villas is often between 20% and 30% of the total, which is significantly higher than the average in Britain. This is a preference which may go back to the Iron Age in this region, since the pre-conquest settlement at Skeleton Green, Braughing, reveals a similar pattern.

Cattle were always the most numerous

animal, however, and in terms of meat value this meant that beef was by far the most common meat consumed on the villa estates and, presumably, in the towns too. The principal pastures would have been in the meadows on the valley floor, which were too damp for agriculture in any case.

Sheep, while providing lamb and mutton, were kept on most estates as a source of wool. Shears found at villas like Harpsden provide reminders of this important aspect of RomanoBritish farming, which contributed to Britain's exports in the Roman period.

To date, the byres and sheds in which these animals were overwintered have rarely been found, perhaps because they lay some distance from the villa or

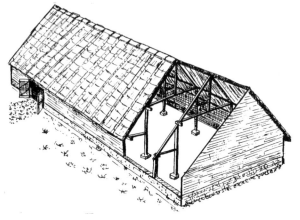

Fig. 5.4 A reconstruction of the Roman barn at Netherwild, Herts.

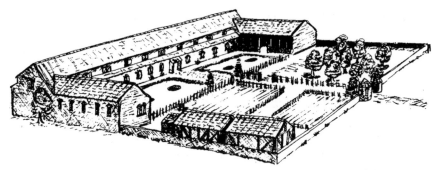

Fig. 5.5 An imaginative reconstruction of the villa at Latimer, Bucks, with its walled garden.

farmhouse, on which archaeological investigation has tended to focus. An aisled timber building found at Netherwild near Mundon, however, may have provided winter accommodation for up to two dozen cattle, with fodder stored either down the centre of the building or in a hayloft overhead (fig. 5.4).

Other outbuildings perhaps used for animal accommodation have been found at the Gadebridge and Gorhambury villas.

The extent to which the Chiltern farmers supplemented their diet and their income by market-gardening is uncertain. The Romano-British period saw the development of various aspects of horticulture, and vegetables like carrot, cabbage and celery,

and fruits such as cherries, plums, pears and apples are known.

There are some hints of vegetable and fruit-growing on the Chiltern estates. Walled enclosures like those at Latimer and Totternhoe would be suitable for this purpose (fig. 5.5), and at Latimer traces of bedding trenches for vegetables were discovered within the enclosure. The discovery of pruning saws and knives and of a variety of spade-irons at several villas provide supporting evidence for gardening and fruit-growing (fig. 5.6).

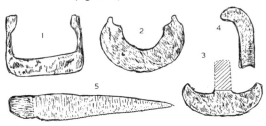

Fig. 5.6 Roman gardening tools from the Chilterns. 1–2: spade blades; 3: turf cutter; 4–5: pruning knife and saw.

A Chiltern Farm

Within this general pattern of farming in the Roman Chilterns each villa estate reveals the particular preferences of its owner and its adaptation to the immediate landscape and resources in which it was situated. We can perhaps best appreciate this by looking briefly at one such estate in more detail.

Gorhambury villa was built on the site occupied by a successful pre-Roman farm, about a mile to the north-east of Verulamium. It stood on a spur of pebbly clay and sand, surrounded on three sides by clay with flints, and by chalky loam and alluvium on the valley floor to the east.

The villa stood inside a ditched enclosure of Iron Age origin and, as it was built at the end of the first century, consisted of six main rooms and a cellar, and had front and rear corridors. In the same enclosure stood a buttressed granary, a small bathhouse and a timber-framed outbuilding of uncertain use. An outer enclosure, also of Iron Age origin, contained further timber outbuildings.

Towards the end of the second century the first villa was replaced by a new house, which provided a similar range of accommodation but included a simple integral bath-suite. Both the bathhouse and the granary in the inner enclosure were now demolished, leaving a simple outbuilding, perhaps a store, standing near the house.

In the outer enclosure, however, important changes took place (fig. 5.7). Nearest the villa were two timber-framed buildings, one perhaps a workshop and the other possibly a house for the bailiff or farm manager. Near the gateway at the opposite end of the enclosure stood a large aisled barn, a circular hut and a new bathhouse. The last was clearly located for the use of the workers on the estate. The rest of the outer enclosure seems to have been given over to a series of paddocks and animal pens.

This complex of buildings and enclosures was the focus of an estate whose boundaries can only be guessed at. Using the evidence of other nearby villas, of topography and of the medieval estates in the area, the excavator of Gorhambury has suggested its total estate may have been around 2,500–3,000 acres (1,000-1,200 hectares). Between 400 and 750 acres (180-300 hectares) of this may have been arable, and

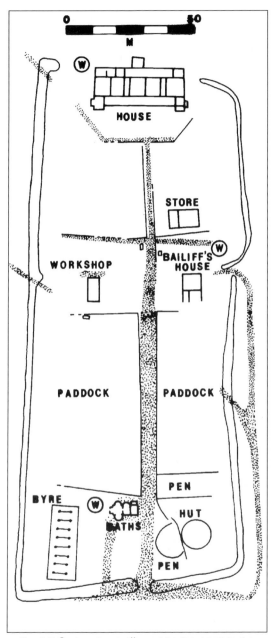

Fig. 5.7 Gorhambury villa and its farmyard in the third century.

several hundred acres pasture. The bulk of it would have been scrub and woodland. The way in which this area was exploited by the farmer is reflected in the buildings, tools and organic remains found in the excavations.

No less than six ploughshares were found (fig. 5.8), and several ox-goads. These, together with the evidence of the granary and a late third-century corn-drying oven, confirm that the arable was probably extensively utilised. The aisled barn seems to have been used partly for housing oxen and partly as accommodation for farm-workers (perhaps the ploughmen), and it is thought that up to six oxen were stalled at one end of the barn. In that case we might envisage these plough teams being able to plough up to 200 acres (80 hectares) of land in the ploughing season each year.

Charred remains of crops show that wheat (emmer, breadwheat and spelt) dominated the cereal crop at Gorhambury with very little barley being grown. Initially much of the crop seems to have been stored on site – in the granary – but unless arable farming declined dramatically in the later Roman period, the demolition of the granary before AD 200 presumably indicates that thereafter the surplus corn was sent immediately to market.

Manuring the arable with both human and animal dung was probably an important factor in maintaining the productivity of the

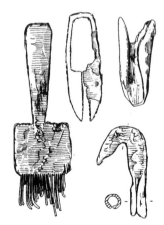

Fig. 5.8 Wool comb and shears, ploughshare and reaping hook from Gorhambury villa.

soil, and the dominance of cattle in the animal population of the Gorhambury estate was, therefore, beneficial to the arable regime. In numerical terms cattle seem to have made up about half of the farm stock, and sheep and pigs about a quarter each. In terms of meat value, this means that cattle were by far the biggest providers, but study of the animal bones suggests that the cattle may have been kept primarily for dairy produce, with meat and hides as secondary products.

Similarly, although a wool comb and shears were found amongst the farm's ironwork (fig. 5.8), sheep seem to have been reared at Gorhambury as much for mutton as for wool, to judge by the age at which they were slaughtered. Pigs, on the other hand, are unequivocally meat producers, and at Gorhambury a good number of them were slaughtered young. They were notably more numerous in the first and second century at Gorhambury (when they represented about a third of all the stock). Since this coincides with the period when two successive granaries were in use, it is just possible that they were being intensively reared on grain at this time. On the other hand no

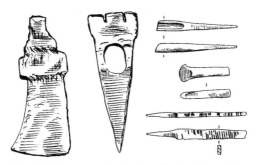

Fig. 5.9 Carpenters' tools from Gorhambury villa.

pigsties have been identified, and there was certainly extensive woodland in which they could have been run.

The woodland was another resource which the farmer would probably have exploited commercially as well as for his own needs. With Verulamium only a mile down the road constantly needing wood for building work, Gorhambury was ideally placed to keep the high cost of transporting heavy timbers to a minimum. Many wood-working tools – an axe, adze, plane blade, file or rasp, gouge and chisels – were found in the excavations, though most of these may well have been used by the estate's carpenter in everyday maintenance and repair (fig. 5.9), in the same way that blacksmith's tools and smithing debris reflect everyday activity on the farm.

Nevertheless, the estate at Gorhambury was in an advantageous position to market its produce to Verulamium, and there can be little doubt that on an estate of this size a considerable surplus could be generated in both corn and animal products to provide a profit for the farmer. This profit could be used both to maintain and improve his villa residence and to support a life-style that reflected a willingness to adopt Roman tastes and fashions.

Romanisation in the Chilterns

The villa house was itself, of course, the most permanent and tangible expression of romanisation. Even in the most basic villa the Roman farmer had the benefits of simple innovations that were unknown in pre-conquest buildings (fig. 5.10).

Hard clean floors of mortar or concrete, tiled roofs and glass in the windows were all improvements, but so was the privacy accorded by solid walls, rooms for separate functions and corridors which provided access

63

Fig. 5.10 A reconstruction of the modest villa at Lockleys, Herts.

to individual rooms. Once the farmer built a hypocaust to provide heated rooms in winter, and a small bath-suite or free-standing bathhouse (fig. 5.11), then additional comforts were on offer. This was an entirely artificial living environment, and it was made even more so by the provision of patterned and decorated mosaic floors and painted walls and ceilings.

Most of the excavated Chiltern villas have proved to have had mosaics, even though most of them have been very badly damaged, and painted wall plaster is commonplace. These furnishings were partly for the benefit and pleasure of the farmer and his family, but no doubt also intended to impress neighbours and friends, invited for dinner in the villa's dining room or *triclinium*.

The tableware on such occasions would be a mixture of locally produced and imported pottery, glass and bronze vessels. Glossy red-glazed samian pottery from France, was a favourite throughout southern Britain and turns up in all the Chiltern villas. It was imported by the boatload into London, and crates of it would have been transported up Watling Street to sell in the shops and marketplace at Verulamium.

Most of the smaller bowls, plates and cups were plain, but the larger bowls in particular were decorated with moulded scenes taken from Roman mythology or showing events in gladiatorial games (fig. 5.12). How many of the villa's inhabitants would have been familiar with the mythology is uncertain, but many of them would certainly have visited the amphitheatre outside Verulamium and seen gladiatorial combats there.

Alongside the samian dinner service, glass bowls, beakers and

Fig. 5.11 The bathhouse of the Dicket Mead villa. The stoke-hole is in front, and behind it is the hot room, with a small apsidal plunge bath to the right.

sauces (very much an acquired taste!) were only widely adopted after the conquest.

Along with these changes or additions to the diet there appears to have been a new interest in herbs and spices as food flavourings, most clearly attested by the widespread adoption of the heavy grinding bowl, the *mortarium*. A small number of these found their way into Britain shortly before the conquest, but after AD 43 they had become commonplace equipment in Romano-British kitchens, and

flagons from the Cologne region were found in many of the Chiltern villas. The owner of the Park Street villa had even acquired a fine glass bowl from Alexandria, decorated with papyrus plants.

The food and drink served in these containers were, for the most part, home-grown on the estate, but surviving fragments of amphorae attest to the arrival of wine, olive oil and fish sauces from the countries around the western Mediterranean and sometimes from further east. The native farmers had acquired a taste for wine in the pre-conquest years, but olive oil and fish

Fig. 5.12 Fragments of decorated samian bowls imported from France showing gladiatorial combat.

were being manufactured in large numbers in the later first century.

The easy, simple way by which to pay for all these new luxuries – from bathhouses and mosaics to amphorae of wine and crates of pottery or glass – was with cash. The extent to which the British adopted the use of coinage for everyday transactions is still disputed, but it is difficult to envisage an endless exchange of products where so much trade and purchase seems to have been going on.

Certainly, coinage was known and used by the villa owners and some of our Chiltern villas have yielded considerable quantities – over 300 coins at Gadebridge and Hambleden, and nearly as many at Gorhambury. Why other villas like High Wycombe and Lockleys should have yielded only a handful is uncertain, but it is more probably to do with the extent of the excavations and the vagaries of discovery than any underlying difference in the way money was used on the different estates.

When the Chiltern farmers went into Verulamium, they had ample opportunity to spend cash generated from the sale of their produce. Although only a few stretches of the high street of Roman Verulamium have been excavated, this limited sample reveals the usual dense concentration of shops and taverns. At one point 13 shops were crowded into a frontage only 65 metres long.

But the town provided farmers with other opportunities both for spending and for displaying their new tastes and interests. If they were worried about the weather and the crops, a forthcoming journey or their health, they could make offerings in whichever of the half dozen temples in the town was dedicated to the appropriate deity. To relieve their gloom they could visit the amphitheatre or perhaps attend a political satire or a musical performance in the theatre. In all of these public places they would indulge in practices which, though they might have echoes of life in the times before the conquest, would have been particularly Roman in both their architectural setting and their presentation.

There would also be more private business to transact in Verulamium, which would again emphasise the influence of Roman practice on their own way of life. It would be in Verulamium that they would find the mosaicists and wall-painters with whom to discuss their new home improvements, or the hypocaust engineers to plan their new heated winter living room.

If they were ill, they could visit the doctor or even obtain the services of a surgeon, while inflamed or sore eyes could be treated by an oculist. A serious illness might lead them to the door of a lawyer to supervise the making of a will, but it was more likely that a farmer would need his services in disputes over land boundaries or possibly taxation. While the former could be tried under Celtic law, if it came to court, the latter would certainly be a matter for Roman law, and a knowledge of Latin would be useful. As a landowner and very possibly a member of the *civitas* council, a farmer would need more formal education than in earlier days and almost certainly would have ensured that his children received a proper education. Teachers at primary and secondary level would have been found in a town the size and status of Verulamium, providing tuition in maths and Latin.

The extent to which the British adopted Latin is again a matter of dispute, but in our Chiltern villas there are indications of its usage. Since the British Celts appear to have had no written language, the appearance of *stili* (writing implements to use on waxed wooden tablets) and seal-boxes (used to seal a document when it was finished) at villas like Gorhambury, Gadebridge and Hambleden, as well as at small towns like Braughing and Baldock, is significant (fig. 5.13). So too is the discovery of a broken inkwell at Latimer, a rare piece of evidence for documents written on vellum or parchment rather than on wooden tablets.

It is interesting to see, too, how often graffiti (scratched words and messages) occur on the side of pots in the Chiltern villas, for these are probably the work of servants or farm-workers rather than the farmer himself and suggest that even the lowliest of the British made some attempt to use Latin.

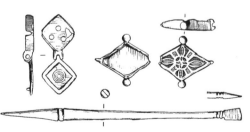

Fig. 5.13 A stilus *(pen) and two seal-boxes from documents found at Gorhambury villa.*

Many of these graffiti are just a single word or number, often referring to the contents of the vessel on which they are scratched, but a few, like the pot dedicated by Regillinus at Dunstable and an incomplete inscription found at Enfield, are more ambitious.

The commonest graffiti are probably personal names, however, and these provide an interesting reflection of romanisation. 'Antonius' from Hambleden villa, and 'Datius' from Harpsden, are two clearly Latin names, while a gentleman dedicating an offering at the rural temple at Barkway prefixed his Latin names 'Censorinus Gemellus' with a first name abbreviated to 'Dum', which was almost certainly Celtic. More interesting still is the man who dedicated another offering at Barkway. He records his name as 'Tiberius Claudius Primus' (fig.

Fig. 5.14 An inscribed votive plaque from Barkway, Herts, dedicated to Mars Toutatis by a freed slave called Primus.

5.14) and he is a former slave – a freedman – whose master, Tiberius Claudius Attius, must have been granted citizenship early in the Roman occupation, and who we can safely assume was himself a man of romanised tastes and attitudes.

The offerings from Barkway must come from a yet undiscovered rural temple of the so-called Romano-Celtic type. These temples were places where similar Roman and Celtic gods were brought together and worshipped as a single deity: they were thus powerful forces for the integration of Roman and native culture. The dedications and a bronze statuette from Barkway indicate that this temple was dedicated to Mars, who was here identified with the Celtic gods Toutatis and Alator. Like many Romano-Celtic temples, it also appears to have served as a convenient place of worship for devotees of more than one god: another offering here shows Vulcan, patron god of blacksmiths, appropriately carrying hammer and tongs.

Another rural shrine lay just across the *civitas* boundary at Harlow, fifteen miles south-east of Barkway, but westwards in the heart of the Chilterns such temples are scarce. Roman remains on the high ground at Frithsden near Ashridge might belong to a temple, but only one certain example has yet been discovered, at Wood Lane End (Hemel Hempstead). This temple incorporates a mausoleum and stands in an enclosure with a small bathhouse. A further building perhaps used by a guild of worshippers stands just outside the enclosure. The whole complex is impressive but something of a mystery. No votive offerings of any kind have been found. The incorporation of a mausoleum into a temple is unusual, and the indications are that the temple and its ancillary buildings were little used. Built in the early second century, it was abandoned and probably deliberately demolished by the start of the third.

The Chilterns in the Third and Fourth Centuries

At the beginning of the third century the Chilterns must have seemed a prosperous part of Roman Britain. Verulamium had recovered from the fire that had destroyed about 50 acres (20 hectares) of its town centre in the mid-second century, and several of the villas had been renovated, improved or extended in the years either side of AD 200.

It may have been a feeling of civic wellbeing and pride that decided the council in Verulamium to front their existing earth rampart defences with a stone wall, and to build impressive masonry gateways across Watling Street, and two monumental arches, probably to commemorate the town's original defences and municipal charter. But such works would have cost large sums of money, and they came not long after the emperors Septimus Severus and Caracalla had each raised army pay by 50% within the space of a decade or two.

The people of the Catuvellauni may, therefore, have found themselves facing very large increases in taxation by both central and local government in the earlier third century. This might explain the apparent abandonment of some villa houses at this time, as Chiltern farmers found they could no longer afford to maintain their country residences. At Boxmoor the villa house was abandoned some time after AD 211, and Gorhambury suffered a similar fate at some time in the early decades of the third century.

It is just possible that more dramatic evidence of the hard times on which some local people had fallen at this time comes from far away on Hadrian's Wall. Here, outside the fort at South Shields, was found a tombstone in memory of a lady called Regina, who had died at the age of 30 (fig. 5.15). She was the wife of a Syrian merchant Barates, who supplied standards to the military. But the tombstone says that she had previously been Barates' slave, and that she was a Catuvellaunian by birth!

Fig. 5.15 The tombstone of Regina, a Catuvellaunian woman, married to a Syrian merchant living near Hadrian's Wall.

Through the third century economic conditions deteriorated rather than improved. Political instability led to a series of Gallic usurpers, who established their own 'empire' which included Britain, and this caused uncertainty. Together with rapidly increasing debasement of the coinage, there was a collapse of confidence and a spiral of inflation. Many landowners, who may have owned both a town and a country house, found it increasingly difficult to maintain both and had to choose which they would temporarily abandon. On present evidence some chose their town house, and others their villa. Villas like Lockleys and Saunderton were certainly in disrepair in the late third century, and both Hambleden and Latimer were almost certainly abandoned for a short time.

Only after the collapse of the Gallic empire, the restoration of Roman authority and the issue of reformed coinage did confidence return, early in the fourth century. Extensions were built at several villas, many had new hypocaust systems, and others had new mosaic floors.

Latimer was not only re-occupied but saw the addition of two wings of

Fig. 5.16 The steps into the fourth century swimming pool of the Roman villa at Gadebridge Park.

rooms, new hypocausts and an extended bath-suite, and the creation of an enclosed garden at the front of the house. The most remarkable development was at Gadebridge villa, where a swimming pool over twenty metres long was constructed (fig. 5.16), and a whole new wing of accommodation added to the house.

Swimming pools are rare in Roman Britain, and the Gadebridge pool is the largest known – even bigger than those at the legionary baths at Caerleon and attached to the temple of Sulis-Minerva at Bath. Two smaller examples may be recognised at other Chiltern villas, at Great Wymondley and High Wycombe.

The sudden abandonment or severe reduction of villas like High Wycombe, Latimer and Gadebridge in the years around AD 350 are therefore something of a surprise. Whether they should be associated with the confiscation of property which followed the attempted usurpation of Magnentius in AD 353 is uncertain, but the usurpation was symptomatic of the unsettled times which set in again in the mid-fourth century and which were to lead to Rome's final withdrawal from Britain.

Chapter 6

Into the Dark Ages

Keith Branigan

Increasing assaults on the coasts of Britain culminated in the so-called Barbarian Conspiracy of AD 367, which saw the coastal defences overwhelmed and raiding parties of Saxons and Franks on the rampage in south-east England. London is said to have been besieged, but whether the raiders reached Verulamium is unknown. Thereafter, however, villas increasingly show signs of disrepair and lack of maintenance, perhaps indicating that the raids had shaken the confidence of the villa owners, who began to move back into Verulamium for greater security.

At Totternhoe, for example, disintegrating tessellated floors were clumsily patched with mortar and then eventually covered with a coarse concrete floor, as living rooms were turned into storerooms or animal sheds. At Saunderton rough walls of chalk were used to buttress collapsing masonry. Latimer villa, which had been drastically reduced in size around AD

350, went through a long period of decline, as crude repairs were made to walls and floors, and more and more rooms went out of use. At Gadebridge the demolition of the villa in the middle of the century was followed by continued occupation of a two-roomed cottage with just a bedroom and livingroom-cum-kitchen (fig. 6.1). Something similar eventually replaced the ruined villa at Totternhoe.

In each case it seems clear that, although the villa house was allowed to fall into disrepair while

Fig. 6.1 The two-roomed cottage occupied in the later fourth century after the Gadebridge villa was demolished around AD 350.

Fig. 6.2 The wall trenches and post-holes of a long timber building erected just outside the villa enclosure at Latimer after the villa was abandoned.

perhaps occupied by the farm bailiff running the farm for the absentee owner, the villa estates continued to be farmed. Even when the main houses had finally become completely ruinous, farming activity continued. Similarly the iron-working settlements at Cow Roast and Foxholes seem to continue to function until at least the end of the fourth century.

Thereafter dating is difficult because coinage and imported goods were no longer being brought into Britain. Troops had been withdrawn from Britain to defend Italy from barbarian attack, so less coinage was needed to pay the depleted garrison. Equally, there was less demand for imported goods and a greater threat to sea transport in bringing them to Britain. By AD 406 the British had elected their first short-lived emperor, and by AD 410 Rome had effectively recognised that it could no longer defend or control Britain. The whole administration and economic system was therefore collapsing rapidly.

In these turbulent times the Chilterns seem to have fared reasonably well. Verulamium continued to be occupied, and some sort of administrative authority was maintained there at least until the end of the fifth century. In the valleys the old villa estates presumably began to lose their cohesion as units of ownership, but the land was still farmed. At Latimer good fortune preserved a stratified sequence of four timber-framed buildings belonging to the post-villa period (fig. 6.2), showing that small cottages were still being built and lived in within the Chiltern heartland well into the fifth century, if not beyond.

VERULAMIUM MUSEUM

The visible remains of Verulamium are well worth a visit. Because St Albans developed mainly on the hill overlooking the site of the Roman town, much of the latter has been preserved and some monuments are still visible. These include the theatre and foundations of some nearby shops, a good part of the city walls, and a room with a mosaic floor in one of the town houses. The theatre is one of the few Roman theatres in Britain, with banked seating facing the stage; it was build around AD 140.

The main museum building, situated inside the Roman town, has a wonderful collection of Roman material from the town. Apart from a wide variety of artefacts of every kind, there are recreated Roman rooms and some of the finest mosaics and wall plasters outside the Mediterranean.

There is a special programme of activities for children and every second weekend Roman soldiers are on hand to explain their armour and equipment. Anyone interested in Roman Britain should visit Verulamium and its museum.

There is a second museum in Hatfield Road, which houses the material from the medieval town of St Albans. There you can see how the town grew up around the abbey and how people lived and worked in the Middle Ages.

The bulk of the archaeological collections held by the museums are from the Roman city of Verulamium and the medieval town. They cover both the everyday and exotic. The museums are also the repository for published and unpublished material covering both Verulamium and St Albans.

Both these museums are worth visiting.

FURTHER READING

You can read more detailed accounts of the Roman archaeology of the Chilterns, and of the wider Catuvellaunian territory, in:

K.Branigan   *Town And Country: The Archaeology of Verulamium and the Roman Chilterns* (Spur 1973)

K.Branigan   *The Catuvellauni* (Alan Sutton 1985)

The best account of Verulamium is:

Rosalind Niblett   *Verulamium: The Roman City at St Albans* (Tempus Publishing 2001)

Detailed reports on specific sites at Verulamium include:

S.S.Frere   *Verulamium Excavations* Vol.1 (Soc of Antiqs 1972)

S.S.Frere   *Verulamium Excavations* Vol.2 (Soc of Antiqs 1983)

I.Stead and V.Rigby   *Verulamium: The King Harry Lane Site* (English Heritage 1989)

R.E.M. and T.Wheeler   *Verulamium, a Belgic and Two Roman Cities* (Soc of Antiqs 1936)

Individual villa reports include:

K.Branigan   *Latimer: Belgic, Roman, Dark Age and Early Modern Farm* (CVAHS 1971)

D.Neal   *The Excavation of the Roman Villa in Gadebridge Park* (Soc of Antiqs 1974)

D.Neal   *The Roman Buildings in the Bulbourne Valley* (reprinted from Herts Archaeology, 4, 1976)

D.Neal   *Excavation of the Iron Age, Roman and Medieval Settlement at Gorhambury* (English Heritage 1990)

Discussions of the small towns of the area can be found in:

B.Burnham & J.Wacher *The Small Towns of Roman Britain* (Batsford 1990)

C.L. Matthews   *The Roman Cemetery at Dunstable* (reprinted from Bedfordshire Archaeol. Journal, 15, 1981)

GLOSSARY

basilica	The central administration offices, usually situated in the main town square or *forum*.
cavea	The auditorium in the theatre.
civitas (pl civitates)	An area of local government – roughly equivalent to a county.
colonia	A settlement of legionary veterans.
curia	The hall where the town council met.
forum	The town market square.
insula (pl insulae)	A block of land bounded by streets. Roman towns were usually laid out in a grid system.
lorica	Body armour.
macellum (pl macella)	A market place.
mortarium (pl mortaria)	A bowl for grinding corn.
municipium	A town with this official status – the origin of our word 'municipal'.
stilus (pl stili)	A sharp pointed instrument for writing on wax tablets.
temenus	The precinct or courtyard of a temple.
vallus	A donkey-driven machine used for reaping.

THE CHESS VALLEY ARCHAEOLOGICAL AND HISTORICAL SOCIETY

The Chess Valley Archaeological and Historical Society was founded in 1963 by a handful of enthusiasts with the aim of studying and promoting local archaeology and history. The practical work of the Society began with the excavation of the Romano-British villa at Latimer. An account of the excavation was written up and published by the Society in 1971 and is still a standard work of reference.

The 1969 the Society conducted an investigation of Stratford's Yard, Chesham, a site to which it later returned for further excavations. The site revealed unexpected evidence of mesolithic activity in the heart of the modern town, and large quantities of worked flints and microliths were recovered. Society members also participated in the excavations at Pann Mill, High Wycombe.

Surveys of archaeological sites have been carried out at sites which include Bray's Wood, Whelpley Hill and Grove Farm – all in the Chess Valley Area. Regular field-walking has further helped to reveal the true level of prehistoric activity in the area. This is an ongoing programme.

An active Records Group is transcribing the volumes of the Chesham Parish Register, which give an insight into the lives and occupations of the past inhabitants of the town and its surrounding villages. These volumes have been published up to 1760. Again this is ongoing – and plans are in hand to extend this to the Chesham Manorial Court Rolls.

As exemplified by this little book, the Society is active in the field of publishing and a list of the books currently in print is given overleaf. A monthly programme of talks is held every winter open to members and non-members and there are visits in the summer.

Recently the Society has introduced a bursary for the younger members of the community (aged 16-22) to enable them to participate in a training dig. Finances (and book sales) permitting it is hoped to continue to award this on an annual basis.

As this book is going to press, the Society is in its 39th year and, sadly, some of the original enthusiasts have passed away. However, as old faces drop away, new people join and the Society continues to expand.

Other publications from the Chess Valley Archaeological and Historical Society

Lady Elgiva by Dr A J Baines   £3.75

Register of Births and Burials for the Parish of Chesham 1743-1760 and Marriages 1743-1754 (March)   £6.00

Register of Births, Marriage and Burials for the Parish of Chesham 1730-1742   £5.00

The People of Chesham, their Births, Marriages and Deaths, 1637-1729   £10.00

Also available on microfiche

The Parish Registers from 1538-1742   £12.00
NB These include the first volume transcribed by J W Garrett-Pegge

In addition the Society publishes an annual Journal, *Chess Valley*. Free to members – non-members   £1.00

All of the above can be obtained from your local bookshop, or from the Society's Publications Secretary, Lena Woldemariam (email lena.hwm@virgin.net) or at one of the Society's meetings.